Praise for
TAROT TRIUMPHS

"There are dozens of books about the Tarot and not all of them tell us anything new. Cherry Gilchrist's *Tarot Triumphs* is among those few that open up uncharted areas and throw a revealing light on what we may think is all too familiar to us. It is a work of insight, passion, and practical engagement that can inform its readers' understanding as well as their lives. One doesn't need a fortune teller to predict that its future looks promising."

—GARY LACHMAN, author of *The Secret Teachers of the Western World*

"*Tarot Triumphs* is simply the best Tarot book I've ever read. Accessibly blending a lifetime's Tarot experience with historical knowledge, personal engagement, creative imagination, esoteric wisdom, and sound common sense, it's equally well-suited to introduce newcomers and to provide fresh stimulation for long-time Tarot users. It seems clearly destined to be a classic."

—PROF. GREVEL LINDOP, poet and author of *Charles Williams: The Third Inkling*

"*Tarot Triumphs* delightfully initiates us into the procession of the Tarot de Marseilles trumps, helping us to wisely read its reflections in the Fool's Mirror. How wonderful to be immersed in such mature and practical Tarot writing!"

—CAITLÍN MATTHEWS, author of *The Complete Arthurian Tarot*

"Cherry Gilchrist's *Tarot Triumphs* is an excellent book for beginners who want to learn to use the Tarot of Marseilles for divination. Unlike most books for beginners, her book is firmly grounded in the actual history of the Tarot and the fact that the trump cards originated in Renaissance Italy as illustrations related to triumphal parades. She also provides valuable insights into the folk traditions that helped shape the cards and their use, based on her observations of traditions in Italy, China, and most of all Russia. Experienced readers will find something to learn here as well."

> —ROBERT M. PLACE, author of *The Tarot: History, Symbolism, and Divination* and the creator of several Tarot decks

"A fresh, bracing, and inspiring look into the Major Arcana. The Fool's Mirror in particular is the most sophisticated and profound Tarot layout that I have ever seen."

> —RICHARD SMOLEY, author of *Forbidden Faith: The Secret History of Gnosticism*

"Although directed towards those starting their own Tarot journeys, *Tarot Triumphs* is an enjoyable and informative read for Tarot veterans as well."

> —THALASSA, founder, Daughters of Divination, producer, San Francisco Bay Area Tarot Symposium (SF BATS)

"A richly textured book that combines fascinating personal experiences with a lifetime's research and wisdom—a must-read for the Tarot beginner or enthusiast."

> —LYN WEBSTER WILDE, author of *Becoming the Enchanter*

TAROT
TRIUMPHS

✦ TAROT ✦
TRIUMPHS

Using the Marseilles Tarot Trumps for Divination and Inspiration

CHERRY GILCHRIST

With illustrations by
ROBERT LEE-WADE

WEISER BOOKS

This edition first published in 2016 by Weiser Books, an imprint of
Red Wheel/Weiser, LLC

With offices at:
65 Parker Street, Suite 7
Newburyport, MA 01950
www.redwheelweiser.com

ISBN: 978-1-57863-604-4

Library of Congress Cataloging-in-Publication Data
Names: Gilchrist, Cherry, author.
Title: Tarot triumphs : using the tarot trumps for divination and
    inspiration / Cherry Gilchrist ; with illustrations by Robert
    Lee-Wade.
Description: Newburyport : Weiser Books, 2016. | Includes bibli-
    ographical references.
Identifiers: LCCN 2016019923 | ISBN 9781578636044 (6 x 9 tp :
    alk. paper)
Subjects: LCSH: Tarot.
Classification: LCC BF1879.T2 G533 2016 | DDC 133.3/2424–dc23
LC record available at *https://lccn.loc.gov/2016019923*

Cover design by Jim Warner
Tarot illustrations by Robert Lee-Wade
Interior by Maureen Forys, Happenstance Type-O-Rama
Typeset in Monotype Modern

Printed in Canada
MAR

10 9 8 7 6 5 4 3 2 1

*To all members of the Saros Foundation for the
Perpetuation of Knowledge—past, present, and
future. And in particular to those who have
been my fellow travelers on the path.*

The innocent Fool holds up his mirror to the heavens. In the patterns captured there, he can see the imprint of cosmic purpose and read the events that are coming to pass.

—Advice on divination from a master of Tarot

CONTENTS

Introduction . . . . *xi*

Chapter 1: Enter the Triumphs 1

Chapter 2: The Tarot as a Method of Divination . 25

Chapter 3: Taking On the Tarot 53

Chapter 4: The Wandering Fortune-Teller . . . 77

Chapter 5: Becoming the Diviner—
Grasping the Fool's Mirror 93

Chapter 6: A Search for Order and
Meaning in the Fool's Mirror 173

Chapter 7: The Fool's Mirror Layout 195

Chapter 8: Managing the Reading 231

Chapter 9: The Fool Leads Us Further 249

Acknowledgments 267

Notes 269

Glossary 293

INTRODUCTION

To set the scene for this book, I would like to reveal something of my own interest in divination as a background to my study of Tarot over the decades. Looking back, I see that divination has cast a kind of silvery, delicately woven net over my life since a very early age, connecting experiences and events in a way that I didn't always perceive at the time. Sometimes the connecting threads were fine as gossamer, while other times they became strong lifelines, giving me guidance and support at difficult moments. I see, too, that although in some ways this has been a journey into the unknown, to a land that lies beyond our everyday world, it has also been a discovery of what was waiting for me there already.

I have always been drawn to divination. As a child, I diligently counted my prune stones after school pudding to see whom I would marry, and I gleefully made folding paper fortune-tellers, in which you could scrawl all kinds of possible fates for your friends. In my teens, the desire surfaced to know more about astrology, dream interpretation, and fortune-telling. This was before the new wave of interest in magical subjects, so there was not much material readily available. On holiday with a friend and her family, in a rented cottage in Wales, age thirteen, I pored over a moldy volume of dream interpretations that I'd found in the bookcase there, my chief entertainment during a week of rain. I begged to be allowed to take it home. Quite reasonably, my friend's mother prevented me from doing so on the basis that the owner might be fond of the book herself. Later, I got my mother to buy me a fortune-telling teacup that we saw in a junk shop—one where little card images are scattered on the china, to be interpreted through how the tea leaves fall—though I never did manage to work it out properly. As for astrology, at that time I could only find very superficial magazine columns to work out what sun signs my friends and I were born under. But I had a kind of instinctive feeling that this all made sense. I was less interested in knowing the future than in discovering how to penetrate this otherworld, the place from which these magical messages seemed to come.

I believe that I was predisposed to seek out such ways of divination. Somehow, I knew that there was an overall validity to divination, even if it could appear in such watered-down, faintly ridiculous forms. There was never a time when I didn't accept that such things could be true. I groped my way toward this world, little by little to start with, and then entered it with full force when I encountered Tarot for the first time, as I shall describe in the opening chapter of this book.

Perhaps for many of us the interest in divination is in fact latent, and it is just a matter of awakening it with the right stimuli. Deep down, we may have traces of knowledge of ancient pathways of wisdom that have been trodden over the ages. It may take time, though, for us to decipher the clues, and for conditions to be right so that the door will open fully for us. But this door may always have been partly ajar.

And so my involvement with divination grew, from childhood games to a serious interest in Tarot and astrology. I have read cards and horoscopes over many decades, and for a while I was a professional astrologer with a practice and even a sun sign column of my own (the latter rather against my better judgment, since sun sign columns are huge generalizations compared to the complexity of the individual horoscope). I do Tarot and astrology readings sparingly now; there is a natural evolution in our interests, and mine are focused more at present on distilling the experience of divination and seeing how it may be set within the nature of consciousness and be a part of our hidden potential. In this book, I hope to bring together the best of both worlds: the practical, experiential approach to divination, combined with the wider context of spiritual understanding, as they are linked together through the powerful images of the traditional Tarot cards.

My recent research has opened up more fascinating trails to follow in the wider field of divination. Over a ten-year period, I made many field trips to Russia to investigate folk traditions, including old divination practices; the cultural outlook there is one where myth, divination, and psychic powers are seen as coexisting quite naturally alongside more scientific or intellectual thought processes. It is a refreshing change from the view that is prevalent in the West of assuming that so-called irrational beliefs must be proven before they have any validity. I have written about these and other Russian customs in *The Soul of Russia*, also known as *Russian Magic*.

Even more recently, I was introduced to the Kuan Yin oracle in the authentic setting of two of her dedicated temples in Singapore and Penang. In terms of Chinese oracles, I had long been a user of the I-Ching; but now I found that the compassionate, maternal quality of the goddess Kuan Yin offered a wonderful counterpart to the

I-Ching, with its more stern, male, and Confucian pronouncements. Kuan Yin also has much to offer in terms of bridging cultures East and West, since her influence spread right along the Silk Road into the West, merging with the Christian portrayal of Madonna and child. I have in my study a beautiful white porcelain statue of Kuan Yin, made in a particular region of China, as it has been in the same way for hundreds of years, as well as a bamboo Kuan Yin oracle pot with its one hundred sticks of fortune, and a guide to her pronouncements, given to me in her temple.

The range of divination practices seems to be almost endless, but in fact there are patterns: the spectrum can be studied, and various common elements discerned, as I have written about in my book *Divination: The Search for Meaning*, as well as here in *Tarot Triumphs*. This is something that I ponder over, develop, and refine as I go along. In some views, divination is a thing apart, something to be feared or revered but not studied as a part of human knowledge and experience. My view, tempered by years of my practice of meditation and Tree of Life Kabbalah, is that we can endeavor to understand divination through exploring our own consciousness and that of the greater sphere of life. Philosophy, new science, and religious teachings all have ways of describing this and helping us to understand, but it's work that is never finished; as part of human evolution, we need to make continual efforts to reformulate what is already known, and to communicate our discoveries to others.

This kind of approach has also involved me in the creation of new divination systems. We tend to think of divination methods as being handed down to us coated with a patina of mystery from age-old use, their true origins lost in the realm of myth. This may often be so, but everything has to start somewhere. It was my Tarot teacher, whom we shall meet shortly, who showed me how to make an effective divination system based on the principle of using a set of symbols that is self-consistent. He asked me to write the handbook for a new divination system, known as "the Game of Galgal," and later published as *The Tree of Life Oracle*. Of my own accord, I have also invented a Russian fairy tale set of oracle cards, after immersing myself deeply in this Russian folk culture over a ten-year period.

The Tarot has remained my first love, my entry proper into the world of divination. I knew as soon as I saw its symbols that they would be my companions on the path, and that they would act as the bridge between the everyday world and the magical realm just beyond it.

My role here is therefore as a communicator and interpreter. I do what I can to "bring the sacred fire from the mountain," as I see it, and to light the torch that may help show the way forward. In writing this book, I have also made the decision to name the Fool's Mirror School of Tarot publicly for the first time, drawing together the teachings that I have received and developed under this emblem of divination.

Cherry Gilchrist
Exeter, 2015

TAROT TRIUMPHS

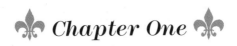

Chapter One

ENTER THE TRIUMPHS

The twenty-two picture cards of the traditional Tarot pack are known both as Tarot Triumphs and Tarot Trumps. Colorful and resonant, these cards form a unique set of symbols that can be used for divination, inspiration, and illumination. The Tarot are called the Trionfi in Italy, the country linked to their earliest-known history, and although they have been allied with the four-suit pack of playing cards for much of their existence, they stand apart as an independent set of cards. It is the Triumphs that form the focus of this book. Although "Trumps" is more commonly used, I have chosen to single out the word "Triumphs" because it connects us with a particular kind of spectacle that was current when Tarot first appeared, and which may shed light on the birth of Tarot itself.

THE TRIUMPHAL PROCESSION

We are about to meet the Tarot Triumphs in the guise of a triumphal procession. These processions were popular in fifteenth-century Italy, somewhat similar to carnival parades as we recognize them today, providing a form of street theater with exotic performers and floats passing by. They were accompanied by music and dancing, and enjoyed by people of all classes. But the triumphal processions also had a more exalted purpose, as they included tableaux that portrayed allegorical and cosmological themes. This was a type of renaissance effort to depict the world in all its glory, embracing both sacred and secular knowledge. All this was revealed, often to celebrate weddings or feast days, in a succession of magnificent emblems, a burst of color and spectacle. The triumphal processions also embodied the notion of "trumping"; each successive figure or display in the procession trumped the one that came before it in terms of moral superiority, spiritual value, or just the social order of the day. It had its roots in earlier Roman parades, where a virtue trumped a vice, Death trumped worldly success, and an emperor trumped a slave, for instance.

Tarot historians suggest that these Italian processions may have played a part in the creation of the Tarot, since they accord with the time and place of the earliest Tarot decks known to us. Some specific emblems are found in both contexts, such as the Lover, the Chariot, and Death.[1] Likewise, the concept of Trumps applies to both the parades and the pictorial cards, even if trumping applies more to games played with Tarot than to its use for divination purposes. The processions are unlikely to be the sole source of Tarot, but there certainly seems to be a link. And this aspect of Tarot history is well worth pursuing, as it indicates how some of the Tarot scenes may once have been viewed as life-size moving spectacles, which would have created an intense experience for onlookers. Very shortly, I will suggest that we try this out for ourselves.

MEETING THE TWENTY-TWO TRIUMPHS

The Tarot Triumphs are evoked three times in this book. We shall meet them first of all in this imaginary public spectacle as it might have taken place on the streets of Northern Italy more than five hundred years ago. When we visualize them as large-scale and gloriously majestic figures, this keys us into not only the power of their images but also a significant cultural event that may have played a distinct part in the history of the Tarot.

The second time we encounter the Triumphs as a sequence is in chapter three, as a set of cards rather than a moving tableaux. Here you can find keynote descriptions and interpretations of each card, accompanied by thumbnail images. These serve to set up the basic meanings of cards for Tarot readings.

The third meeting with the Triumphs is in chapter five, where there is an in-depth investigation of each card, including its history and a close examination of the detail of its imagery. A full-size, line-drawn illustration of each card, commissioned especially for this book, accompanies each description. These broader discussions encourage us to see the apparent paradoxes and mysteries in the cards, which will further a deeper and more intuitive form of Tarot interpretation.

I hope that this threefold approach will offer you different ways to experience the symbols of the cards by giving food for the imagination as well as useful background knowledge. You may find it helpful to know this now so that you can navigate the book as you wish, or cross-refer between the chapters.

TRIUMPHS AND TRUMPS

I use the terms Triumphs and Trumps interchangeably throughout this book in referring to the twenty-two cards of the Tarot Major Arcana. The words are linked linguistically: the Italian word *trionfi* translates into "triumphs" and "trumps" in English. They have different shades of acquired meaning, but I have chosen to combine them here to celebrate their earlier origins in the melting pot of fifteenth-century Italy, both as processions of Triumphs and the earliest gorgeously hand-painted decks of Tarot cards. And, of course, "triumph" is something that Tarot is and does; it triumphs through its powerful images, its persistent survival through the centuries, and its capacity to instruct and illuminate those who study it.

WATCHING THE PROCESSION

Tarot, in the light of the triumphal procession, may be seen as an act of theater, its images a kind of magical performance moving through the sequence of the cards. We can turn this historical link with the triumphal processions to our advantage, and use the context imaginatively, as a way of discovering the kind of impact that these magnificent Tarot Triumphs could have when paraded through the streets.

So let us now step back in time to witness a spectacle of Tarot Triumphs moving through a city street in fifteenth-century Italy. Our procession happens in the hours of darkness, which accords with how some of these spectacles were presented, and for us it intensifies the vision of the Tarot scenes as they pass by, portrayed as characters and tableaux.

As you read the description of the procession, I suggest that you place yourself in the jostling crowd, on a city street, hundreds of years ago. Visualize how these twenty-two images appear from out of the warm darkness. Let these vivid, otherworldly scenes fill your imagination as they pass by, one by one.

Keep your pack of Marseilles or traditional Tarot cards at hand, if you have them, to refresh your memory of each image. If you don't yet have these, and are new to Tarot, then you can look ahead to the main illustrations of the Tarot Trumps in this book first, and quickly acquaint yourself with the sight of them. Or you could even just allow the words to paint the pictures for you, with no external reference at this stage. No matter how familiar you are with Tarot, it helps to renew the link between Tarot and the imagination in this way so that the images stay alive in your mind. Seeing them here as life-size, active figures will paint the picture afresh. There is always further to go in understanding the Tarot symbols.

THE PAGEANT OF THE TRIUMPHS

"Make way! Make way!"

The crowd is hushed. There's an expectant silence as people press against each other, lining the street. The night is dark, but a few torches blaze down the thoroughfare, creating flickering pools of light surrounded by deep shadows. Everyone is squeezed in together, so that the rough cloth worn by working folk rubs against the finer textiles of the merchants and their ladies, and expensive perfumes mix with the smells of sweat and unwashed clothing. The stones of the city walls radiate the heat absorbed by day, making it uncomfortably warm for those pressed up against them at the back.

The burly heralds announcing the procession carry torches too, swaggering purposefully, swinging the flames toward anyone who dares step forward too far.

The low sounds of breathing, rustling, and murmuring are growing in intensity, breaking into an excited chatter. But then this too falls away as drumbeats begin to sound. Solemn, resonant beats coming ever closer. It's here! It's beginning! Children are hoisted onto shoulders, and everyone cranes forward to see. The drummer, all in black, heads up a small marching band, which now strikes up strident tunes on pipes and shawms.

Then there is a creaking of wood, a rumbling of wheels, and the first of the Triumphs appears. The crowd cheers. The parade of Triumphs has arrived.

The Magician, clad in brightly contrasted parti-color tunic and breeches, stands tall as he is borne aloft on the first wagon of the procession. He holds a wand in his left hand, a small golden ball in his right. His broad-brimmed hat gives him a jaunty and somewhat outlandish look, as though he brings his conjuring from an exotic kingdom. On a small table in front of him lie the tools of his calling—dice, knife, cups, ribbons. Will he perform sleight of hand, magic tricks to delight the spectators tonight? He picks up a little ball, holding it delicately between forefinger and thumb, and a knowing look appears in his eye.

Before the people in the crowd can speculate what he will do now, the next Triumph is upon them. A woman with a lofty headdress sits enthroned, a cloak around her shoulders and a book placed open on her lap. *The High Priestess* is all stillness, all wisdom. She sits in front of a portal draped with curtains; directly behind her is stretched a kind of veil, which appears to mask the entrance to an inner sanctum. Her silence and stillness affect those who watch. If only she could read out a few lines from that book; each person in the crowd feels it would tell them exactly what they need to know.

Another female figure follows, also on a throne, but bearing the crown, orb, and shield of *the Empress*. She is regal, haughty, and she glances sternly around the crowd, quelling the questioning chatter. She wears a gold chain around her neck, and on her shield is the imperial eagle, which brooks no argument. Perhaps she is pregnant? Her stomach swells a little; she may be producing an heir. Only some people notice this, and they smile secretly to themselves. Even monarchs must make love and perpetuate their family line. This way, they can feel a kinship with their Empress. She casts her glance to one side now, either immersed in her own thoughts or disdaining to look upon commoners.

In quick succession comes her consort, *the Emperor*. The Empress is powerful, but he is even more so. He has a more finely carved throne, a heavier chain and pendant, and a more brightly burnished eagle. He sits sideways so that onlookers can see his commanding profile and observe how his look is fixed steadfastly ahead of him. He holds his mace proudly aloft. He is authority, over temporal matters at least, and represents rule. His rule is iron, but sure; for his people feel instinctively grateful, as no one likes a vacillating leader.

The Pope follows after, seated and arrayed in sacramental robes. His processional triple cross is grasped in his left hand. Several disciples kneel at his feet, gazing up at him as he holds up his right hand in benediction. No one can fail to sense the intensity of his pose, and the stillness of the disciples is almost painful, given the posture of supplication that they must hold and endure. But he too engenders a sense of security, of teaching transmitted down the ages and given with a blessing.

There is a change now, from figures of authority to that of *the Lover*: a young man flanked by two women, with a cupid figure hovering above him, surrounded by a starburst. One of the women is a beautiful maiden; the Lover has his arm around her, and she places a hand on his heart. But he looks toward the other, who is crowned with laurel leaves and wears a more severe expression. She places a hand on his shoulder as a reminder, or perhaps an admonishment. The cherub is ready to fire his arrow. Which woman should the young man choose? Will he follow his head or his heart?

The young prince now approaching does not need a carnival float to convey him, for he is the master of *the Chariot*. His horses bend their proud necks and pull his canopied chariot smoothly, wheels clattering over the ancient paving stones of the street. But where are the reins? If they are there, they are invisible to ordinary eyes. One hand holds a golden staff; the other casually but regally rests on his hip. He surveys the crowd thoughtfully; he means to go somewhere, and no one should stand in his way. The crowd is not comfortable under his gaze.

Justice follows, seated with her sword and her scales. Her eyes are wide open, and she stares clearly and impartially straight forward, as is her custom. The scales are perfectly balanced, the sword perfectly upright. Not even the greatest powers in the land will meddle with her, and she will see that justice comes to all. Although she is severe, the bystanders are confident in her powers. The tiniest tilt in the scales must be corrected, and she is ever vigilant to keep them that way.

Standing upright, holding a lighted lantern, *the Hermit* is both imposing and humble. He wears a rough, hooded cloak and is bearded, with long locks. In his other hand, he holds a wooden staff. These are the symbols of his role. He does not have the ceremonial regalia of bishops or kings, but he has his own authority and wisdom, derived from the life of poverty and contemplation. Some in the crowd would like to bring their questions to him, to benefit from his insight. They know that hermits, though solitary, can be consulted. He is also a reminder of the need for charity that should be given not only to the poor but also to those who pray for the welfare of humankind.

But just before the tenth Triumph appears—what is this? *The Fool* zigzags through the wagons, a bundle tied to a stick slung over his shoulder and a walking staff in his hand. He is never still, never of one mind. Sometimes he capers, sometimes he imitates or taunts the crowd. At other moments, he breaks your heart with his ragged poverty, the rent in his breeches, and the sad expression on his face. And then he laughs again, and the moment is forgotten. A little dog runs alongside, jumping up and tearing at his trousers. Is this comic, or tragic? No one really knows. If he can wander with his worldly goods tied up in a bag, then perhaps anyone can: freedom is not so far away after all.

Then *the Wheel of Fortune* rolls into view, a giant wheel ridden by strange animal-like figures, one ascending, one reigning at the top, and the third descending head-down. The Wheel offers a lesson so that all may observe just what the rotation of Fortune means. It takes us from humble beginnings, to ruling triumphantly as king—on certain feast days, as the crowd knows, anyone can be crowned king or queen for a day according to custom—to sad descent into obscurity, stripped of royal trappings. It was ever thus for money, birth, and worldly success. Luck may not be fairly distributed, but everyone experiences both happy strokes of luck and sad misfortunes too.

Next comes *Strength*, a mature and beautiful woman, with hat and cloak and flowing robe, who is prizing open the jaws of a lion. Or, she may be closing them, some say. This is theater, the crowd knows, but oh how realistic it looks! They hold their breath, wondering if she can sustain her gentle mastery over the fierce beast. How does she do this with only a woman's strength? Has she charmed the lion, perhaps? But those who observe closely see that she does this by gentleness; she is firm, but not forceful. The lion obeys her command and remains obedient to her touch.

Now it's the turn of *the Hanged Man*, a young man suspended upside-down from a cross pole. A ripple runs through the crowd: What is he doing like this? Is he dead? Has he been hung as a criminal or a traitor? But look, he is quite serene. He is balanced, one leg crooked behind the other, arms neatly folded behind his back, eyes gazing forward. There is sporadic, relieved laughter when they recognize him as a skilled acrobat, one of the rope and pole dancers who gladden the streets sometimes. But nevertheless, his frozen posture casts a sinister shadow on their reckoning. To be turned upside-down like that would be uncomfortable, to say the least, and your sense of security could fall away in no time.

There is a collective gasp of horror as *Death* proceeds into their midst. He is a grinning ogre of a skeleton, the mighty sickle in his hand. Perhaps a man in a black costume has been painted in the manner of a skeleton? Or perhaps it is a real skeleton—they say you can come across these in the old grave pits. Neither possibility is reassuring. His image is well known, but still everyone tries to escape it; no one can, though, for Death is implacable and inevitable. But wait—there are plants and flowers beneath him among the litter of heads, hands, and feet that he has severed. What is this new life that is growing?

Who comes afterward? It is *Temperance*. There is some relief, as this winged angelic figure follows, a five-petaled flower bound to her forehead. She casts a steady glance to the side, as if concentrating on her task as she pours water, or perhaps wine, from one jug into another. Temperance, moderation: everyone knows the meaning of that. Or do they? There is something miraculous here, for the water or wine never ceases to flow, and it is a two-way flow between the jugs. How can that be? Temperance is about keeping away from excess, but here the resources seem to be infinite.

But then *the Devil* appears, and all recoil. He has leather wings, a horned headdress, and a sharp-looking sword, as well as clawed feet and a naked, ugly, half-female chest. Two little devils are chained to the pedestal he stands on, where their master is acting as though he were king of the world, one taloned hand raised up in sovereignty. Some who are watching know, though, that the best way to dispel the Devil's power is to mock him. Chants, ribald comments, and even a few missiles are hurled, causing the accompanying torchbearers to threaten the crowd and restore order. It works though, for the Devil has passed by.

Here is a wonder, *the Tower* struck by lightning. A tall tower stretches up high, borne along as a tableau, but its splendor has been breached. A jagged flash of lightning is represented, piercing the crown of the tower, which is broken, half hanging. A continuous patter accompanies the float, as small stones spatter down from the gaping hole at the top. Two men seem to be falling from the tower, already almost down to the ground. This is a marvel indeed, and some of those present remember tales of towers being struck to the ground—even church towers—due to the pride of man. But it can also be imprisoning to stay cooped up in such a tower, and perhaps there is some value in being released from its narrow walls.

What follows is balm to the soul. *The Star* appears: in the background, a great, shining star is surrounded by seven smaller ones, while in front, a naked lady kneels on the ground by a pool of water. Behind her are two trees, with a bird perched upon a branch. Its beak is open, as though it has a message to deliver. The lady pours water from two jugs into the pool. She must be an emblem of life, of healing, and a sign that all is well. Perhaps she can reach those waters only when she is stripped of all her worldly clothes and appearances; she seems, in any case, to point the way to another land where fresh discoveries can be made.

And then the mood shifts again, as a great tableau portraying *the Moon* glides among the bystanders. It has no human content, unless you count the face of the Man in the Moon. It reveals a landscape of a haunting kind. Two towers flank the horizon, and in the foreground two dogs bay at the moon while great drops of moon dew fall to the earth around them. In front lies a pool, in which rises a giant crayfish drawn upward by the moon's magnetic rays. This is a fine, fantastical scene, and yet it arouses a faint sense of unease. Everyone knows that the tides of the moon affect the moods, the blood, and the energies of human beings. Its changing face has a power that can provoke strange dreams. Nothing is fixed under the moon's rays.

The Sun comes next, and the onlookers feel thankful for what is so bright, so welcome and familiar. A huge, radiant sun with a majestic face represents the light of day, and under it two young boys who could be twins stand in front of a wall, their arms around each other. They are naked, apart from their loincloths. A simple innocence emanates from them. Some of those present long for that simplicity of childhood, while others look forward to the return of the sun the next day. All recognize its light and warmth. The Sun is our birthright, and it brings confidence in our place in the world.

The Fool, meanwhile, is still on the go, prancing merrily and then resuming his more somber tread. Perhaps he is a kind of pilgrim. He is on the move—that is certain.

The procession is nearing its end. Now that the celestial bodies of the skies have been portrayed, it is time for *Judgment*, that which comes at the end of time itself. Man should look up to the heavens, but he should not forget his end. High up in the sky, an angel can be seen blowing a trumpet hung with a banner. Below, three human figures emerge from a pit, summoned by the Last Trump, as this call is known, from their newly opened grave. They adopt postures of reverence, with hands placed to pray. They have died, but they will rise again. The mood of the crowd is sober but cautiously hopeful.

The very last Triumph is *the World*, who appears as a dancing girl clothed only in a long, filmy scarf floating from one shoulder and holding two batons. Life appears again in its fullest form, as a dancer poised in an oval wreath, treading her dance with grace. Around the wreath, placed at the four corners, are the four Holy Creatures, which many watching recognize as the Evangelists too: the angel, the eagle, the ox, and the lion. But everyone, even those from far away who have other faiths, can see that this is the holy dance of life, the soul of the world that includes all the creatures of the earth. It is a wondrous scene, and a fitting conclusion to the pageant.

A peaceful mood descends upon the crowd, and when the heralds announce that the show is over, and the band plays a last plangent chord in the distance, everyone departs with a good grace. They will talk about this night, and its marvels, for months to come.

THE SOURCE OF THE TRIUMPHS

Were some of the Tarot images drawn from the processions of Triumphs? The historical evidence is indicative, though not conclusive. But whether or not our Tarot cards of today crystallized as part of this medieval pageantry, the experience of visualizing the images in this way, as a procession of larger-than-life scenes, is a powerful one. I believe that this is likely to be one of the historical strands that led to the formation of the Tarot pack, even if it doesn't account for all the Triumphs. When I first read about the possible link with triumphal parades, it struck me as absolutely right in the imaginative sense too. One of my own early encounters with the Tarot, which I'll describe shortly, was of watching huge, colored images of the Tarot projected successively onto a screen, an occasion that made a deep impression on me. And if we put ourselves in the place of those onlookers, many of whom would have been illiterate, with little color or imagery in their daily lives, we can imagine how intensive the experience might have been for them.

So recreating an imaginary procession of the Tarot Triumphs is not too far-fetched as a historical idea, and it may have a kinship with the way the symbols were perceived at the time they emerged. However, there's no attempt on my part to say that the Tarot set as we know it is derived from a "lost" triumphal procession, complete with all twenty-two emblems. This could perhaps be the case, but from what we know of early Tarot history, its images seemed to be in a fluid state at its inception, and it took some time for the different variations to be crystallized into a more or less standard form. But in terms of the types of scenes in a triumphal procession, and perhaps some of the specific images used, it may be a link to how Tarot itself was first conceived.

It is this visual impact that draws most of us to the Tarot today. We are lured in by its imagery and the intensity of its symbolism; it has a kind of theatricality. The cards also create a sense of mystery, of a meaningful sequence that may point the way to a school of knowledge behind the construction of the images. Views vary as to what these inner teachings may be, and we may never know whether the cards came together as a result of deliberate embodiment of such teachings, or whether they are the result of a merging of folk wisdom and classical learning, fashioned over time by usage. Their exact history is still elusive, though much has been discovered over the last fifty years, as we shall see in the next chapter.

Tarot is a living tradition, and my own place in this has been shaped by my encounters with certain individuals who have mastered the Tarot, as well as by my own research and practice with Tarot over the years. Just as Tarot follows a path of evolution, so too is our personal relationship with Tarot likely to develop as time goes on. It is a never-ending process: as I write this book, new ideas arise, and my sense of the Tarot quest becomes exciting once more. Earlier, I hinted at the association of the Tarot Fool with the role of pilgrim, and perhaps he represents the questing soul in all of us, a figure forever exploring what the cards of the Tarot have to offer.

I invite you to join me in the quest for knowledge of these twenty-two remarkable Triumphs, and to learn the Fool's Mirror system of divination.

THE FOOL'S MIRROR

As the book unfolds, I will explain the Fool's Mirror approach to Tarot, which has largely been shaped by my early encounters with Tarot and, to a very significant degree, by the person who created the term "Fool's Mirror" to symbolize the process of divination itself. The theme of the Fool's Mirror, including a unique layout using all twenty-two Tarot Trumps, will be developed throughout the book, starting with a definition of the term in chapter two. For now, I would like to describe how the living tradition of Tarot drew me in through my interaction with three knowledgeable Tarot masters. This is a way of naming those people who initiate you into the life of the Tarot, whether through a fleeting chance encounter or a more profound and prolonged training period.

JO: MY FIRST TAROT MASTER

My acquaintance with the Tarot began in 1968. I was nineteen years old, a student at the University of Cambridge in the United Kingdom, and I had come to America for the summer vacation. Several of us had flown in for a three-month idyll of free rock concerts and hanging out in the sunshine. But it was the year after the Summer of Love, and the culture that had seemed so innocent then now began to take on a more sinister tone, with riots in Chicago and bad LSD trips beginning to take their toll on the flower power generation. I soon realized too that our student habits of wearing long hair and vintage clothing, considered harmless British eccentricities at home, antagonized the more conventional side of American society. I thought I was streetwise after teenage years in Birmingham and a year of counterculture in Cambridge, but it was a rude awakening. We had tear gas thrown at us on the streets of Berkeley, and we were hauled off to the police station for fingerprinting in Reno. Then, in Mexico, I was involved in a terrifying car accident in which I thought I was going to die. I had only minor injuries, but the experience was a profound shock that changed my way of thinking forever. I could not go on just drifting along on the stream; I needed to address the big questions of what life is about.

So it was in this troubled yet formative time that I first saw the Tarot cards. I had already resolved to start a meditation practice when I got back to Cambridge in the fall, and not long afterward I would encounter Tree of Life Kabbalah, a path that I have followed in one form or another ever since. Astrology would also come onto the agenda, but at that time I knew nothing more than a few sun signs picked up from magazines.

When I first set eyes on the Tarot cards, they blazed a trail like a comet in my imagination. They hinted at another world beyond our normal senses, and I knew instinctively that the Tarot could lead me into this realm.

My first Tarot master was a young man called Jo. He lived in Berkeley with his wife, Peggy. As with most twenty-something American men whom I got to know at that time, Jo also lived with the shadow of conscription. Being married made him less likely to be called up to serve in Vietnam, but this was still a possibility. Jo and Peggy were trying for a baby in order that his name would slide even farther down the list. One of his friends was drafted while I was there, that summer, and I saw the shockwaves that this produced. Other young Americans were fleeing to Canada and Italy to avoid the draft, some of them never to return. So Jo and others lived on the edge. This was another factor that impinged on my protective bubble; we had no such threats or wars in the United Kingdom at that time.

Jo spread out the pack for me. It was a revelation. He used the Rider-Waite Tarot pack, created by author A. E. Waite and artist Pamela Colman Smith at the beginning of the twentieth century. It is probably the most popular pack in use today, apart from the traditional Tarot of Marseilles. Every card, including the suits of the Minor Arcana, is represented as a pictorial image and is rich in symbolism, drawn partly from the symbolism and teachings of the Hermetic Order of the Golden Dawn. It is a very vivid, very bright pack. I fell in love with it. I felt that each card was a portal through which I could enter a magical world.

Jo's reading has gone deep into my memory—so deep that I can't actually recall what he told me! But it changed my perceptions radically, and from that point on the Tarot was imprinted on my psyche. Jo had a seriousness that was sharpened by the American situation, I believe, and he read the cards not just as a fanciful tryst with esoteric imagery, but as a vital tool for life in uncertain times.

THE NATURE OF A TAROT MASTER

Jo thus effected my initiation into Tarot. A Tarot master is, I suggest, someone who acts either as your first true point of contact with Tarot or as a teacher of Tarot at any given moment along the way. Maybe the person is an expert, maybe not. But he or she does know something, and if through that knowledge and living contact your own connection is sparked, then this is the work of a Tarot master. Tarot is a living tradition, and coming to it through someone who is involved in that chain of transmission creates a special understanding of the cards, which will probably color and illuminate your understanding of the Tarot for all time. Of course, this is not the only way that an individual encounters Tarot in a meaningful way. I don't doubt that for some people the pack of cards itself, or a particular book, may also open the door to a true encounter with Tarot lineage. If this book can achieve that for anyone, I will feel honored to be a link in the chain of transmission.

In terms of a personal meeting, I suggest that it is appropriate to be grateful for such a contact, though it might not always be an entirely comfortable interaction. A Tarot reading, for instance, can shake up our preconceptions and reveal truths we have previously been unwilling to accept. But it can nevertheless open a doorway and be the start of inner growth. I acknowledge this kind of contact with gratitude and hope that I in turn can help to open up a path for someone else.

We can't plan or manufacture this kind of initiation, though, because it's dependent on time and circumstances. As a nineteen-year-old at the crossroads of my life, I was in prime position for such an experience. Jo, whom I had previously looked on as a cheerful acquaintance of little importance in my summer travels, then became the first Tarot master in my life. We have not been in touch since that summer, and he probably has no idea of the impact this reading made on me. Jo gave freely of his knowledge, which is the best anyone can do, and I benefited. He took me through the crack between the worlds. The cards imprinted themselves upon my mind and became lifelong companions.

So, my advice is to cherish what experiences and knowledge you may acquire in this way. They form the basis of your own story with the Tarot. Each person's story, though, is different, tempered by individual destiny and life circumstances. And as I tell you my own story here, perhaps a little sympathetic magic will come into play and help to trigger special Tarot encounters and illuminations for you too.

FINDING THE WAY

After I returned to England, I tried to find a Tarot pack of my own. It wasn't easy; they were rarely on sale, and one bookshop I approached said that they feared the old Witchcraft Act might be invoked if they dared to display them. Actually, this law had been replaced by the Fraudulent Mediums Act of 1951, but as this gave license to prosecute anyone taking money for deceitful acts of clairvoyance using a "fraudulent device," there was perhaps some reason to believe that supplying Tarot cards could get them into trouble. The fear generated centuries earlier by the witchcraft trials had not entirely evaporated.

The Tarot, as far as I was concerned, was innocent of such taints. I ignored popular opinion and persisted until at last I had one, and then two, Tarot packs in my possession. I now owned both the Rider-Waite pack and the traditional set known as the Tarot of Marseilles. I still have them as part of my collection, well used but intact.

RAZ: THE DARK TAROT MASTER

My second Tarot master was a saturnine and rather sinister man called Raz. I was a second-year student at university, and he looked relatively old and sophisticated to me, though he probably wasn't much over thirty, if that. A friend had put me in touch with him.

"You're interested in the Tarot? Ah, then you want to speak to Raz. He knows all about it."

By the time the meeting was arranged, for some reason in a public hall in Cambridge, I'd learned some unwelcome facts about Raz. "Yes, he's not long out of prison. Got into an argument, and Raz pulled a gun." My friend shrugged nonchalantly, as though this happened every day. (Guns are rare in the United Kingdom, and they are mostly associated with criminals.)

I was nervous and self-conscious when Raz and I met. He looked me up and down, did not seem impressed by what he saw, and began his Tarot discourse. He laid out the twenty-two Trump cards of the Major Arcana in a big circle on the floor, with the Fool at the center. When it was complete, we stood in the middle. There we were, in a large, empty room, enclosed by a magic circle of cards. It was not alarming, but it was eerie. There were no props or decorations to distract us, so the cards would be just what we made of them, right there in that space. As my second Tarot master, I now recall Raz as a dark, forceful character who considered himself an authority.

By this time I had some experience in Tarot, and I didn't want to be considered a complete novice. I felt some resistance as he began to relate his theory of how one phase of the cards led on to another. The twenty-two could be divided into three sequences of seven cards, with the Fool numbered zero as a wild card, free of such constraints. Again, his version has become overlaid with others in my mind; many years have passed, and I recall the quality rather than the detail of what he said. What he did teach me, though, was that there are ways of finding inherent structure within the sequence of Triumphs.

And I also discovered that I could learn from someone even if I didn't like or trust them. Being pushed out of one's comfort zone is often the first real step to learning; America did that for me in general, so that I was open to encountering Tarot, and now my own will and judgment were definitely in uncomfortable friction with an imperious, and perhaps dangerous, man. But his message got through, and he became my second Tarot master. We did not meet again.

GLYN THE WELSHMAN: MY THIRD TAROT MASTER

My third Tarot master appeared in the form of a plump, bearded Welshman of middle years called Glyn. A talk on the Tarot had been advertised in Cambridge during my final year as a student. I was eager to go, having missed an earlier one on Kabbalah and the Tree of Life, also put on by the Society of the Common Life, as this one was. I was now a student of meditation and was beginning to find my way into the spiritual practices that would shape my future path.

During the evening, Glyn projected slides of each Tarot card onto a large screen. The experience was intense; each card had a powerful presence. At the start of the talk Glyn struck me as a strange man, someone who didn't fit into any pigeonhole, but by the end I realized he was an extraordinary man. He showed us that night how the Tarot cards can accord with higher truths, as well as reflect the mundane features of daily life. They are, he implied, sacred glyphs. His words had great resonance for me. The effect was profound, and that night I dreamed vividly, encountering symbols of Tarot and alchemy that I scarcely knew in my waking life. The dream also had great urgency, as though a task awaited me. It showed me that it was time to leave pointless concerns behind and begin a frightening but essential journey toward what mattered, to reach the land that lay across the water, as it appeared in this dream.

Glyn acted as interpreter of my dream when I plucked up the courage to write it down and send it to him. It was the start of an association that would last many years, during which he was a guide to me in matters esoteric and spiritual, especially Tarot and Kabbalah. I use the word "guide" advisedly, since Glyn did not want to be anyone's teacher in the conventional sense, let alone a guru. He was a Hermetic guide in the sense that Hermes Trismegistus himself guides the initiate through different stages of transformation; Glyn's chosen role was to show others the way, rather than doing the job for them. Sometimes he did this through joking, or playing the trickster, or even by being downright rude. Thus, Glyn, as my third and most enduring Tarot master, encouraged me to look further. He operated by throwing out tantalizing fragments, provocative arguments, and enigmatic statements and rarely by giving me all the information on a plate. I had to find out a great deal for myself, and through my own experience.

Much of what I learned from him, and through his guidance, is embedded in this book. I do call him my Tarot teacher in this context too, since he taught me, on a one-to-one basis, the particular layout to which I give pride of place in this book. He also encouraged a questioning approach to the cards, teaching me to dig deep into their meanings and never to take the current fashionable interpretation for granted. In this specific sense he has been my teacher, and my prime Tarot master.

So my perceptions of the Tarot have been greatly influenced by my encounters with these three Tarot masters.

The first, Jo, showed me that Tarot works as a divination system. The second, Raz, taught me that imagination is not enough, and we should think about structure, number, and sequence in the pack, even if there are different ways of arguing the case. Lastly, Glyn revealed that these images can be gateways to the mysteries. These encounters have inevitably shaped my understanding of Tarot and how I shall write about it in this book.

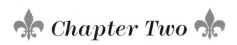

Chapter Two

THE TAROT AS A METHOD OF DIVINATION

Tarot can be used very effectively for divination. If you ask a question of the cards, then shuffle and lay them out in a particular order, some answer is likely to emerge from interpreting that configuration. This requires an understanding of the Tarot symbols, and of the patterning of the layout, but it is a method of divination open to anyone who takes the trouble to acquire this knowledge. In case I seem to be stating the obvious, not everyone has used Tarot for this purpose. Many people have used the pack for card games, and others, particularly recently, study it primarily to develop spiritual or psychological insight. This book, however, is mainly about Tarot divination: that is to say, using the Tarot Trumps as a means to gain access to knowledge that is normally beyond our conscious grasp. In this way, we seek clarity or guidance in the situations of life. It is primarily a search for meaning. Tarot divination can also act as a mirror of the soul, reflecting someone's personal state, including hidden elements that are not usually discernible.

This is the basic concept of how we can use the Tarot for divination. But to set all this in a wider context, let's first explore the idea of divination itself and see how Tarot may fit into the wide spectrum of divination methods. Then we'll take a foray into its history, following an intriguing and often elusive trail back toward its source. All this can only be an overview, within the scope of this chapter; many points are bound to remain unexplored in such a brief exposition. Nevertheless, having some sense of the bigger picture, even in a general way, can deepen our understanding of Tarot too. Seeing Tarot in its divinatory and its historical contexts adds to our appreciation of it. This in turn can increase fluency in using the cards and give confidence when deciding what approaches to employ in Tarot divination. It also helps us to maintain a thoughtful, flexible outlook. Rules tend to become rigid when these deeper sorts of questions are not asked, and then a system is at risk of becoming brittle and losing its inner life.

DIVINATION: A UNIVERSAL OCCUPATION

Divination has been widespread in all times and places, ranging from the ancient method of casting knucklebones to the technical calculations of modern astrology. At all times, in all places, people have wanted answers to their questions. Will it be a fine summer for the harvest? Are the king's enemies plotting to overthrow him? Can I succeed in business? Will I marry this year? Methods have been both simple and complex, sometimes depending on a great deal of learning but often practiced by those in village communities with little formal education. Signs in nature, such as patterns of wind and weather, and the cries of birds, have frequently been interpreted as portents of what is to come. Traditionally, the most serious and complex forms of divination may have been the province of astronomer priests, shamans, or wise women, but almost everyone including children practiced some kind of fortune-telling. My first experience of divination happened when I was about five years old and I joined in the game of counting the number of prune stones left on my plate at school dinner. We chanted "tinker, tailor, soldier, sailor, rich man, poor man, beggar man, thief," and other such incantations, to determine whom we'd marry.[1] I expect that most of you reading this book will remember something similar.

I use the term "fortune-telling" advisedly, since most of these sorts of games are carried out in a rote, mechanical way. Even little girls know that lots of stewed prune puddings will give you lots of chances to bag different kinds of husbands if the first one doesn't please you, but that all these different answers can't possibly be right. Unthinking or repetitious types of divination become two-dimensional; they are at best playful, and at worst ridiculous attempts to determine the truth of what is, or what is to come. The importance, I suggest, is not so much in the method—although that is important, and needs a degree of complexity to be capable of enough variations—but the spirit in which the question is being asked, and the moment of asking it. If divination is approached with full attention and treated as something out of the ordinary worthy of special consideration, then it is more likely to produce meaningful results. In days gone by, diviners held that they were asking the gods for answers, and this was an act not to be taken lightly. They would attempt to approach the act of divination with respect, appropriate ritual, and a pure heart.

THE FOOL'S MIRROR

The Fool's Mirror was my Tarot teacher Glyn's final legacy. For many years, I had practiced Tarot reading, both in the ways he showed me and also broadened by my own research and experience. His approach to Tarot did not have a name until the final months of his life, when I heard him use the term Fool's Mirror for the first time. It was new to my ears, but it made sense of everything that we had worked on over the years. Very simply, the Fool's Mirror is a symbol of divination, a means of capturing the impressions that we hope to interpret. Then, in patterns innocently captured, you can read the imprint of cosmic purpose and events that are coming to pass.

The Fool is innocent and open to all knowledge. Holding up the mirror is the act of divination itself, a conscious act, committed with good intent. Capturing patterns, in specific divinatory terms, is the method and means of divination, whether it is the stars in the sky, the tea leaves in the cup, or the cards on the table. These are "reflected" in the Mirror of the Fool. The success of the interpretation will depend upon the level of understanding of the practitioner—hence the need to learn the language of divination—and on the openness of the questioner receiving the interpretation. The way the Tarot pack falls as it is laid out is one such form of patterned mirroring. The Fool's Mirror is no small or foolish thing, though. It can also be described as the Great Mirror, in which the Fool or the diviner sees all things at the same time.

The Fool's Mirror was the last legacy that I received from Glyn, and it is an image I use now to draw together the strands of my Tarot practice of many years, and the name given to what I now present as the Fool's Mirror School of Tarot. This is the perspective that has shaped this book, and these are the threads of my own experience and understanding. Later, in chapters five through eight, we'll look further into the outlook and ethos involved.

This teaching is not just the product of one man, with the addition of my own views. It is, I believe, "a whisper from the School of Knowledge," as the Zohar puts it.[2]

DIVINATION: THE SOURCE AND THE QUESTION

In essence, divination is the process of asking a question to gain greater knowledge than is normally available to us. But to whom is this question posed? Who or what might produce the answers? In the Fool's Mirror approach to divination, we can call this "common mind," meaning a greater sphere of consciousness and knowledge than we possess as individuals, but one that we can have access to. Naming this source as "common mind" acknowledges a spiritual presence in the universe, which may point the way to the divine origins of life, but the concept is not in itself attached to any one religion or form of deity.[3] It accords to what is needed for any form of serious divination, where we must implicitly acknowledge a higher source, when we seek answers that we cannot find through our everyday powers. It implies a more cosmic perspective; one where the linear forms of time and space may be transcended and glimpses of future events are possible. Skilled insight and individual wisdom can of course bring much to a divination reading, but for the divination to work it has to have this quality of the transpersonal.

It is also important to understand that while divination may be a serious affair, it has its lighter side too. Divination does not in any case provide absolute answers, and while it can inspire a sense of awe, it also has a playful, creative side to it as well. It is like the play of light on water, never providing exactly the same experience twice. Just as the Fool can reflect the naked truth, he also play the clown and provoke laughter or needle us into seeing what lies beneath pretense or pomposity. Just when you think you know him, he changes his appearance and surprises us once more.

This shows up in the way a serious divination reading appears to be telling us something of the truth, but in a manner different from a psychological analysis or the kindly personal guidance offered by a friend. It can bring a sense of "hitting the nail on the head," of penetrating below the surface, but not always in the most obvious way. The reading may offer us surprises and perhaps enigmas that we have to wrestle with and live with over time before they yield their full meaning. Divination symbols have much in common with those in dreams, and they do not always yield a straightforward, logical interpretation.

Overall, divination offers a chance to access knowledge not normally available to us and invites us to transcend at least some of our limitations as individual beings, something that will be explored further in chapter seven. Those boundaries, which normally restrict access to this wider realm, are there for good reason: so that we can act and function in the universe, and have personal identity, rather than being completely subsumed in a greater unity of time and consciousness. But from time immemorial, people have sought to glimpse what is beyond these horizons. Our human capacity can never be as great as universal consciousness itself, but it can certainly be extended. In a way, divination, which through its very name means a connection with the sacred, allows us to read aspects of that universal mind. The act of divination, therefore, brings its own sense of awe and fulfillment. The answers to the questions of divination may sometimes be less important than the experience of attaining such understanding.

THE ESSENTIALS OF DIVINATION

Before we focus specifically on Tarot, it may be helpful to take a further look at the activity of divination overall.

Divination requires a *method*, which usually means choosing or creating a *pattern* to interpret. It is not the same as prophecy, mediumship, or purely psychic perceptions, such as hearing inner voices or seeing visions, although these can certainly overlap with divination.

Divination also, as we have just seen, requires a *question*, which can be anything from "What does this mean?" to "What kind of life will this person have?" Turning this around, we also find that formulating the question for the reading can be an important part of the process. It is all too easy to ask for guidance from divination just on the basis of a longing to be rid of confusion, or to be liberated from an uncomfortable emotional state. Putting words on a question can really help, as a woolly approach to divination is likely to produce a vague answer. "What do you want to know?" is the question that confronts us, and which we must respond to with a clearly phrased question of our own. In my experience, this can often sort out the times that I might really benefit from guidance through divination, as opposed to those when the question is still unclear.

The moment of divination is significant too. At this moment, in this particular conjunction of time and space, a question is asked by this particular person, producing a unique answer. This answer usually needs to be interpreted through the medium of divinatory language. This is done by carefully considering the symbolism in this language and interpreting the answer within the context of the question. Even if, for instance, you consult the Chinese oracle the I-Ching for yourself, the wording that you read in the answer still has to be interpreted and applied to your own specific situation.

Sometimes the timing is a key part of how a particular divination method is practiced. For instance, in horary astrology, the horoscope is drawn up for the precise moment that the question is asked and interpreted accordingly. "Who stole my fish?" is the theme of a horary chart drawn up by the famous seventeenth-century astrologer William Lilly.[4] Lilly wanted to know which thief was responsible for making off with the fish he had bought and had consigned to be ferried up the River Thames to his home. The chart was calculated for the moment he posed the question, not the time of the suspected theft, and by using the divinatory rules applying to a horary chart, he managed to point the finger very precisely at a certain fisherman. The fisherman's house was searched, the fish discovered; to Lilly's great annoyance, part of it had already been eaten! "I found part of my fish in water, part eaten, part not consumed: all confessed."[5]

In other systems, use of rituals and the raising of awareness are seen as helping to create suitable circumstances at this specific point in time to conduct a divination. There can also be ways of showing whether the reading is valid for this moment too; in the Fool's Mirror layout (which we will go into in depth in chapter seven), if the card of the Fool appears in the central line, it means that either the time or the circumstances are not right to proceed. Likewise, when I visited the temple of the goddess Kuan Yin in Singapore, I was shown how to consult her oracle by first casting yin and yang stones to check if the time was favorable to ask a question, before proceeding to shake the cylinder containing the one hundred sticks of the oracle in order to displace the one that would provide my specific reading.

DIVINATORY PATTERNS

There are different ways of capturing patterns in the Fool's Mirror for divination, and here I offer an overview of the main methods involved. These are not the only ways to divide up the cake of divination, and the list may not be completely comprehensive, but it is a useful way of understanding the process.

Free-flowing Movement

Free-flowing movement involves looking for patterns and imagery as they are seen to arise in moving elements, such as clouds, flames, and water, for instance, and reading their shapes and significance. Traditional teachings may offer guidance as to what these mean, or the interpreter may be expected to take a more intuitive approach.

Divination Defined by Direction

Sometimes the specific direction of the movement has meaning; an example of this is bird augury, which was particularly popular in Roman times and was based on the flight path of birds. Another example is that of a Russian folk custom in which a young girl divines the future of a love affair by casting a wreath of flowers into a stream and seeing which way it floats, or even sinks. The dowser's pendulum also works with direction, usually interpreted by whether the swing occurs in a straight or circular movement, interpreted as "yes" and "no," or "here," and "not here."

Arrested Movement

Various divination methods depend upon the moment at which something stops, and the pattern is read for that point of halting the movement. It is a kind of "freeze-frame" approach. This is actually true of the Tarot cards, which are shuffled until the appropriate moment comes to halt, at which point the cards are laid out in their current positions. An astrological birth chart is a kind of arrested movement too, as it is a snapshot of the planetary positions of our solar system at a particular moment in time, as recorded from a particular point on earth. The planets move on, but the birth chart is said to represent the qualities of the individual who was born at that time and place.

Occurrences and Visitations

Sometimes meaning is ascribed to unexpected but significant-seeming happenings—a black cat crossing one's path, for instance, could be an omen of good or ill luck, according to the particular folk tradition in use. Spots and marks appearing on the human body can also be read as indications of the current situation and what is to come in a non-medical sense. Particular manifestations of weather are also understood to be portents in many traditional cultures. Unexpected weather events during ceremonies are often taken as omens, as was the case when a thunderstorm struck during the christening of Britain's Prince William in 1982.[6]

INTERPRETING THE TAROT

What kind of divination system is the Tarot? After a brief look at the context of divination, we move on now to focus almost exclusively on this intriguing set of cards. Tarot comprises a set of images, twenty-two powerful symbols that are very specific but that have an archetypal, universal quality. Almost anyone, from any culture, can pick up the cards and find some recognizable, meaningful symbolism there. The Sun, for instance, as one of the Triumphs, is a real celestial body that all human beings are aware of. There are shared interpretations across the globe: everyone acknowledges that it represents warmth and light, and to many it can therefore stand as an emblem of truth and energy, for instance. But our specific culture and affinities will also shape our perceptions of what it symbolizes. Alchemists look for the image of the sun in their vessel, as a harbinger of the gold they are making; Christians may see Christ as the eternal sun in their lives; and Jungians may greet the presence of the sun in a dream as a welcome sign of individuation.

Here we can see the difference between universally shared interpretations of a Tarot image and the ways in which our cultural heritage, historical knowledge, and specific affiliations will affect our viewpoint. Tarot's specific historical context also plays a part in its interpretation, and as the chapter progresses, we will set more of that in place. In chapter five, too, we investigate specific attributions of the individual Tarot images, after which we will have a more layered appreciation of Tarot, with archetypal, historical, cultural, spiritual, and personal dimensions. This provides a sound basis from which to interpret the cards.

However, you can also add a great deal to your knowledge of Tarot by picking out the contradictions and oddities in the cards. Marseilles-style packs are more or less standard in their imagery, so we can question the makeup of each Triumph. In the case of the Sun again, we can ask: What do the two naked children signify? Why is there a wall in the picture? These are not obvious correspondences with the symbol of the Sun, so it may take some musing to work out why these details are there.

Bear in mind, though, that small details, such as the color of someone's shoes or the number of lines used to depict the folds on a cloak, are unlikely to have an implicit significance and may change from pack to pack, as different makers introduce their own variations in style. I will give more pointers to the significant elements as we go along, especially in chapter five, but it's stimulating and productive to get into the habit of questioning the cards straightaway. See what does not conform with your expectations, and speculate. Pick out any innate paradoxes, consider the cultural associations that may have influenced the image, and ask what those might signify. The Hanged Man, for instance, does not look miserable, dying, or dead in most packs. Why is that? Why is he upside-down, yet apparently happy? (You will find my suggested answer in chapter five.) Learning from other Tarot writers is useful, but learning how to ask the questions and search for answers is the real key that will allow your understanding of the cards to blossom.

TAROT SET AND SEQUENCE

Another consideration to take into account is that of the Tarot as an ordered sequence of twenty-two cards. How the sequence is structured, and whether the current numbering was intended, is open to debate, and something that we will explore more fully in chapter six. What is clear, though, is that as a set of twenty-two, Tarot is a well-defined system, rather than an almost purely intuitive or psychic form of divination, such as gazing into a crystal ball or at patterns of tea leaves. However, although it has some numbering and order, it is less technical and structured than astrology at the other end of the divinatory scale. The power of symbol overrides the possible numerical attributions, meaning that imagination and intuition play a strong part in the process of Tarot divination. We can see this in the way that beginners can produce quite effective Tarot readings, based mainly on making a connection with those symbols. Although longer study will certainly give more depth to their approach, such an initial approach is not possible with horoscopic astrology, which demands mastery of its glyphs, symbols, and structures before an interpretation can be made.

PERSONAL INVOLVEMENT WITH TAROT

Tarot, therefore, is a divination system lying between those systems that use purely free-form images and those that include complex technical data. The way we perceive the Tarot is also a mix of personal response and an understanding of its cultural and mythical content. So overall, Tarot reading offers a chance to practice a balance of intuition and learned information. Keeping that kind of balance is also the best way to ensure that your engagement with the cards is both fruitful and safe. If you simply use set interpretations for Tarot cards, the reading will be dull and mechanical. However, by the same token, relying entirely on intuition to interpret

Tarot can become too subjective a means of divination. And reading Tarot for yourself or for someone close to you may be risky, and sometimes downright dangerous. If each card is an archetype, or some form of deep-rooted myth, then that symbol can take on a kind of power in a person's mind, and its meaning can become distorted by the fears and wishes there.

As an example, I can cite the experience of a friend of mine. She was then in her sixties, and an experienced and sensitive Tarot reader. But she succumbed to the temptation of doing a reading for her daughter, who was undergoing some serious health problems at the time. So the person concerned (the daughter) had not asked for the reading and was not present at the time—two factors that can seriously undermine the basis of the divination. My friend was very worried about her daughter, and when Death came up prominently in the reading, she feared the worst. But, as we shall see, Death is very rarely death in Tarot; it more often signifies the end of the old and the beginning of the new. Indeed, the daughter did not die, and nothing dreadful happened, but her mother remained for some weeks in a state of fear and anxiety, which she could not dispel. Nor, of course, could she talk to her daughter about her fears. So she was in a worse situation than before, and the reading was no constructive help to her or her daughter at all. However strong the pull to turn to Tarot for guidance, the boundaries need to be observed both for our own sake and that of others. We are all likely to make mistakes in this way, but let us hope that we can learn from them.

We therefore need a conscious and careful approach to Tarot. Its symbols are powerful, but by keeping a perspective, studying the background and symbolism of the cards, and doing readings appropriately, we can attain that favorable mix of both learned and intuitive responses to a Tarot spread. This will light the way toward a helpful, truthful reading.

THE HISTORY OF THE TAROT

In the 1970s, not long after I left university, I spent a lot of my spare time researching the history of the Tarot. At that time, there was very little written about this, and there was a particular dearth of serious contemporary research. Plenty of fanciful notions were still in circulation, especially the one ascribing the Tarot to Ancient Egypt, a now thoroughly discredited theory. I dreamed instead about finding its source in a medieval esoteric school, or perhaps as a gypsy fortune-telling system drawn from some ancient, lost mythology. I fought to get permission to study in the British Museum, no easy feat at that time, and I finally entered its illustrious circular Reading Room with little to guide me except for a drive to delve into the symbolism of each card. This research proved fragmentary, but nevertheless it produced some interesting associations that I still apply to the cards, not all of which have been cited by Tarot historians. I will include some of these later, when examining each card in detail, in chapter five.

This period of research wasn't just about wading through books and poring over illuminated manuscripts. I also had the privilege of examining packs of antique cards in the British Museum and other London museums. Although I relish the ease with which we can now find good photos of historic Tarot cards online, nothing can quite compare with handling these old packs. I recall looking at an early version of Waite's Tarot cards. The original printing blocks for these were destroyed in World War II, so today's modern reconstructions do vary somewhat from the first designs. I had a strong sense as I studied them that the colors and meanings of the cards were heightened, and that the cards were imbued with extra, detailed significance that was lost when the printing blocks were reconstructed later. And there was the thrill of holding cards from older decks, often roughly printed and crudely colored, but with a real sense of history to them. They aroused an insatiable curiosity in me at the time. Who used them? Whose fortunes were read? What did the Tarot readers make of the pictures on the cards? The experience of touching and holding these sets of antique cards certainly added an extra dimension to my research.

My quest would not be the same today, as excellent research has been done since the 1980s into Tarot history, and an impressive body of knowledge has been built up. My first forays into the background of Tarot were primitive by comparison, but they did give me a wonderful sense of the mysterious landscape of Tarot history. I also took the opportunity to bone up on the earlier eras of Western esoteric teachings, in particular Rosicrucianism, Christian Kabbalah, astrology, alchemy, and magic. This not only served my broader interests, but it also meant that I could perceive the overall context into which Tarot has fitted with some degree of understanding and objectivity. That is what I aim to bring to this book, even though I am not a specialist Tarot historian as such. And looking at its history here helps us to gain some sense of Tarot's life story, which in turn enriches the way we then interpret and work with the Triumphs.

This brief foray into Tarot history follows the evolution of early Tarot into what we now call the Marseilles Tarot, the most recognizable, popular form of the cards, and the set that is the prime focus for this book.

The origins of the Tarot Trumps are known with certainty to date back to the fifteenth century; there are still some packs of cards in existence from that time, and there are also documented reports of other such sets being made, which have not survived. It seems that the Trumps were initially added to the four-suit playing card pack that was already in circulation. Playing cards are known to have existed in Europe since the fourteenth century and are thought to have originated in China in the ninth century; the old Silk Road trade routes may have played a part in the evolution and transmission of the playing cards, just as they did in transmitting myths, art, and religious ideas. The Silk Road was the way by which not only material goods were transported between East and West, but also cultural concepts.

The earliest Tarot cards that survive come from Italy in the mid-fifteenth century. Several incomplete sets, which were exquisitely painted for aristocratic patrons such as the prominent Sforza and Visconti families, are still preserved. It was initially thought that one very fine deck originated earlier, in late fourteenth-century France, but this pack, still referred to as the Charles VI Tarot, is now more reliably designated as Italian. It was possibly made in Ferrara and is dated to the fifteenth century. Italy thus seems to have played a key role, if not the key role, in launching the Tarot in Europe. The Tarot Trumps known from this time are not numbered, and they are not always named either. Illustrations of many of these early examples are gorgeous and can quite easily be found online.

We do not know if it was only the aristocracy who possessed the first Tarot packs, or whether these fine art cards produced for wealthy patrons were based on other images already in popular circulation. Cheaper woodblock prints of the four-suit playing card deck were certainly on sale earlier, in the late 1300s, and laws passed at the time show how popular these were, as the legislation attempted to halt the rise of card-playing mania among the lower classes.[7] The main spread of Tarot decks to the general population almost certainly came later, in the early seventeenth century, when popular versions began to sell in the thousands. These were usually produced complete with the four suits in packs of seventy-eight cards. (The suits in Tarot have fourteen cards, not thirteen as most modern playing cards do.) By this time the printing press had become established, although most Tarot packs were produced as woodblock prints that were hand-colored. The painting was sometimes very crude, but nevertheless they were vigorous and lively. Even then, the production of playing cards was often governed by legal restrictions and taxation, so Tarot cards could not always be as widely distributed as their makers wished.

Unfortunately, these packs in popular use would naturally tend to wear out, or be lost or discarded, so there are very few packs or even single cards left in existence. Tarot historian Michael Dummett suggests that only three decks have survived out of at least one million Tarot packs in circulation in France in the seventeenth century.[8] This is still enough, however, to see how the prime twenty-two Trump version of the Tarot was shaping up in France and other countries, and for contemporary scholars to distinguish two or three main variants within that evolution. However, our knowledge of the development and circulation of Tarot is still patchy and open to speculation. The story is not over yet, and there is plenty of scope for keen researchers to dig further into its history.

Even the origin of the name is still uncertain. Trionfi (Triumphs) was apparently the earliest name given to the cards, while the word Tarocchi (Tarot) came later, implying the complete card game including the Triumphs. Opinions vary as to the etymology of Tarocchi: it could be an Arabic word, or it may derive from the Italian river Taro, or from an old Italian word *tarrocho*, meaning fool, or even from Barocco, an early term for the Baroque, signifying the extravagant and bizarre.[9]

One issue with defining Tarot history is that it is not just a linear development, but has various offshoots and separate developments during its history. Just as the Silk Road was in fact a collection of branching routes, so Tarot history has its own highways and byways. For our purposes, however, we are following one of the major roads of the historical Tarot trail by focusing on the Marseilles Tarot. The twenty-two cards that I am using in this book became the main established set of Triumphs over the course of the seventeenth and eighteenth centuries and are now thought of as the "traditional" version of Tarot. The generic name for this pack is the Marseilles Tarot, linking it to the place where many of these designs were produced, once Tarot had spread beyond Northern Italy, where its origins are thought to lie. But although Marseilles was one of the centers of Tarot production, this particular design also became widespread over a much bigger region in Europe, appearing elsewhere in France, and in similar or allied versions in Italy, Germany, and Switzerland in particular. There were some standard variations, especially that of swapping the High Priestess and the Pope for Juno and Jupiter in countries where any hint of Catholicism was distasteful. Another common ploy was to print double-ended packs, using just half of the existing image and presenting each picture in mirrored fashion, for the purpose of playing Tarot card games. Naturally, this produces an incomplete and much less powerful version of each Tarot symbol. An elite version of Tarot, known as the Minchiate pack, contains ninety-seven cards and has allegorical allusions; it is more philosophical, and less powerfully symbolic, in my view. And so the variations go on, along with regional and cultural differences. The suits of the actual playing cards have never been completely fixed either, so that the Germans may use leaves, acorns, and bells where French and English players have spades, clubs, and diamonds. Suits accompanying the Marseilles and other more traditional Tarot packs are usually designated as coins, cups, swords, and wands.

Just as the cards had settled into their now recognizable generic forms, the Marseilles deck prime among these, a revival of occultism in the nineteenth century sparked off a wave of new Tarot designs based on personal interpretation or esoteric theory. These sets of cards are usually named after their authors, such as Etteilla, Papus, Wirth, Waite, and Crowley. Then, after the early twentieth century, Tarot production dwindled and it was hard to acquire packs of any description. But in the last quarter of the twentieth century, Tarot fever set in. Hundreds, if not thousands, of different designs have since been created and printed. Many of them bear no relation to the traditional Tarot in terms of their imagery but are named Tarot in a generic way, signifying a meaningful, pictorial deck of cards that can be used for insight or divination. Although I prefer traditional Tarot Trumps, I too have tried this approach and created a Russian Fairy Tale Tarot.[10]

TAROT EVOLUTION

There are leading questions that arise about the origins and evolution of the Tarot, in relation to the search to understand whether the cards arose by accident or intent, and what meaning may be embedded in them. Was Tarot created with intentional esoteric significance, or did it evolve into being considered significant in this way? Was it a product of a "teaching school" or of the folk imagination? Did the Marseilles style of Tarot emerge by accident or by design? Were Tarot cards used for divination right from their earliest appearance? No one can deny that the cards have been used for fortune-telling, but some people question how far back that tradition stretches, and whether the Triumphs have any genuine philosophy embedded in them.

No final answers have yet emerged, but we can consider the possibilities. To start with, we do know that the earliest surviving packs were elaborate works of art, commissioned by the nobility, and these sets weren't identical to one another, although there are strong similarities. Sometimes too there are indications that specific allusions were made to the patron's family. For instance, one version of the Lover card appears to show a specific family wedding in progress, which has been identified as an important alliance between Francesco Sforza and Bianca Maria Visconti. But these variations were most likely created to please particular patrons and do not form the foundation of individual Triumph images.

In any case, we do not know for sure that the story of Tarot started there, with those gloriously painted sets of cards for the nobility. It is possible, for instance, that there were cheaper, popular woodblock packs out there at the same time that have not survived, and that kept more to the basic imagery and sequence of Tarot Triumphs as we know them. Perhaps there could even have been earlier versions of the set of Tarot images portrayed in different media, such as in book or manuscript form, a series of paintings, or even tableaux acted out on the streets. The parade of the Triumphs that we saw in chapter one was an important concept current on the streets of late medieval Italy and stretching back to Roman times. Each successive float or tableau trumped the one before it, which in the case of the Tarot would result in the Magician being trumped by the High Priestess and so on, all the way through to the final Trump of the World, following—rather appropriately—the last Trump of the last Judgment.

These Triumphs on parade showed worldly, moral, and religious emblems, which drew on allegory, history, and Christian teachings for their values. A Triumph procession is described in Petrarch's work *I Trionfi*, dating from the late fourteenth century, which alludes to vices and virtues and draws from popular symbolism in representing the characters taking part in the procession.[11] As we saw in chapter one, the idea of the Tarot Trumps emerging one by one along the city street as a spectacle is a colorful and powerful one, and it does resonate with the kind of images that Tarot embodies. But which came first, and whether the Tarot corresponds exactly to a painted form of the spectacle, is a moot point. We should certainly consider the influence of this kind of pageant, and the motifs it included, but in my view this is likely to have been just one strand of Tarot history.

Tarot, after all, has evolved to become a sequence of twenty-two images that hold together well as a set; they seem to be deliberately chosen, drawn for the most part from classical allusions and medieval imagery, but presented in an original way, and as an apparently meaningful set, not as a random mix of allusions. And they evade attempts to tie them into one specific source.[12] They contain elements of known images, as we'll explore in chapter five, but they have an identity of their own as a set and sequence of symbols. This has led to frequent conjecture that a form of spiritual teaching may well have been embedded in the early forms of Tarot, perhaps a version of Sufism, Kabbalah, or alchemy. This is speculation, but not outlandish conjecture. Or perhaps it emerged from a school of wisdom that has not survived in any other recognizable form.

If Tarot is indeed the product of a teaching system, then what better way of putting those higher ideas into circulation than through a game of cards? It pleases the poorer people, who want some fun, some gambling, and a set of colorful images with a touch of magic. It feeds the aspirations of the nobility, who might consider a gilded pageant of Triumphs in miniature to be a fashionable acquisition in their castles, displayed for after-dinner entertainment. Adding a set of twenty-two cards to the four suits of playing cards already in existence makes for a winning combination. It's possible therefore that this was done deliberately, and that the idea caught on. And as this would be a means of putting old teachings in a new guise, there may be no immediately obvious antecedents. We are left with a collection of images, some of which can be referred to as emblems and motifs from different sources but which have their own sense of integrity and meaning. This is Tarot, which up until the present day retains its aura of mystery and enigma.

We do not know how many steps there were along the way, and whether the troubadours a couple of centuries earlier had a hand in introducing Tarot images, or something similar, to southern France and surrounding countries. Certainly, it's often conjectured that the troubadours' lyrical output was founded in mystical inspiration, imbued with a theme of love and longing, and that their particular brand of mysticism was inspired by Sufism or Jewish Kabbalah.

Or did gypsies play a part, as some conjecture? This is less likely, much as it appeals to many Tarot aficionados, myself included. Romany gypsies are now known to have left India about fifteen hundred years ago, a date rather early to have brought Tarot imagery with them.[13] The images overall have an early medieval to Renaissance feel about them, injected with some strong classical associations. There are no overt Eastern allusions, and Tarot is generally considered to be a European invention, so an Indian origin seems unlikely. It seems more likely to me that the Tarot Triumphs emerged out of a more deliberate attempt to weld a set of images together by people with better access to books and manuscripts than gypsies were likely to have. The gypsies would have been on the move and lacking in formal education. But perhaps gypsy fortune-telling, as the Roma moved around Europe, played a part in the transmission. There is an element of learning to the Triumphs, an infusion of Christian imagery and also of more pagan beliefs, something that could have emerged from several centuries of evolution as images were picked up from diverse sources and gradually blended into a complete sequence for fortune-telling, imbued with folk wisdom; after all, wisdom itself is not the exclusive property of the educated classes.

THE JONGLEURS

I would also like to credit the jongleurs as possible creators or transmitters of Tarot. These were medieval traveling entertainers who could juggle, sing, perform acrobatics, play instruments, act, tell stories, and even tame animals.[14] Their profession overlapped with that of the troubadours or trouvères of southern France, whose poetry and music were on the whole more high-flown, but who shared the roaming, performing, marvel-seeking, and wonder-creating characteristics of the jongleurs.

Although the jongleurs peaked in the thirteenth century and were in decline by the fifteenth century, the period from which we have the first Tarot examples, they were by no means extinct. I have no direct evidence to show that the jongleurs had an early version of Tarot in their possession, but some of the Tarot Triumphs seem to be closely linked to their type of showman activities. At the very least, their work could have provided strong images for some of the early Trumps, as witnessed by the early creators of Tarot at jongleur performances. Or they could have been retained in folk memory as stock images even if the actual performances were not so prevalent anymore, just as we still have strong and rather romantic images of the highwayman, pirate, wandering minstrel, and May Queen in our heritage, even if they no longer exist in real life in that form.

The Fool (or Jester) and the Magician are strong candidates for jongleur figures for obvious reasons of clowning and performing magic tricks. So is the Hanged Man, taking my preferred interpretation of him as an acrobat demonstrating his balancing tricks. Strength, the woman taming the lion, could be linked to the female jongleurs of the travelers' bands, whose acts included animal taming. The World, a scantily clad dancer, is also a possibility. Death appeared in similar guise in play-acting and spectacles of the time, particularly in the Dance of Death scenario, so he could have been part of jongleur repertoire. And perhaps a toppling Tower and a rotating wheel might have been part of the props, or, at the very least, a feature in the stories and plays offered. The Wheel of Fortune could have been a gambling game, offered at shows just as people still pick out lucky numbers from a revolving drum at fairs today. The cultural memories of jongleurs and their performances would be likely to linger on after their high point of fame and provide atmospheric, recognizable images that would work well in the Tarot mix. At any rate, whether jongleurs played a part as folk memories, popular performers, or even creators of the first Tarot cards, I put them forward for consideration in the early history of Tarot. The vernacular also brings us more to the heart and spirit of Tarot; although its history and imagery place it among the nobility as well, I believe Tarot embodies a folk culture that may have been there all along and was not just a place where Tarot ended up in later centuries.

THE LONG PROCESS

As our knowledge of Tarot history grows, different theories will probably continue to emerge, and opinions will not be united anytime soon. Finding out what came first, which elements were involved, and how they came together is a hard task. My guess is that there was some kind of conscious infusion of a teaching tradition into the Tarot cards.

One objection to such a theory is that the pack didn't apparently emerge fully formed, or take unique shape in the same version of the Marseilles pack that we know now. But with the development of an occult or esoteric system, this may often be the case anyway. Astrology took about two and a half thousand years to crystallize into the main form as it is now practiced. It was a long, slow, process— not simply trial and error, but more like a big thought process during which the idea was developed and gradually refined. It can take many minds, and a lot of time, to bring an idea fully to fruition. The initial impulse can also give rise, eventually, to different traditions, such as those of Indian and Western astrology, which use a different zodiac system. All of this is akin to the evolution of folksong and folklore, which is aided by countless individuals over the centuries repeating, varying, and honing the material until ultimately you have a ballad or a myth or a calendar custom that has a sense of magic to it, and is well-smoothed like a stone washed in a stream over the years. And these will have their own variants too. There may have been some kind of conscious creation to start with—a bard who wrote a song, for instance—but the real work is done in the transmission, which alters, distills, and forms something that is durable and meaningful to those of that culture. So there can be individual input, but the realization is accomplished by many, ending with a version that has something of the human soul in it and speaks to us across the centuries.

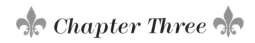

Chapter Three

TAKING ON THE TAROT

Tarot cards have been shaped by generations of human imagination and have acquired their own unique mystical and magnetic presence. We do not know exactly how and why they emerged, but they have certainly come to represent a kind of magical heritage. For hundreds of years, people have pondered the cards, read fortunes, and played games with them; they have recreated and varied the images and gleaned insights from them. Whether or not there was one person who invented the pack to start with, the human psyche, or "common mind," has done its work. If there was ever a single original pack, it has been altered, smoothed, honed, and tested over the centuries. We only need to think of the different artists and engravers working on all the different packs, creating their own version of the designs, each interpretation maybe just a little different from the last. Imagine, too, all those generations of colorists applying bright brushstrokes to the woodblock outlines, painting with intense concentration in humble ateliers to bring the cards into their full glory. Each of them may have dreamed about the cards in their own way and applied the colors just a little more inventively to leave their personal mark.[1]

And then we can recall the wide range of people who have used Tarot: nobles, common folk, merchants, gypsies, and travelers, all with their packs for game-playing, gambling, fortune-telling, and perhaps also for deeper reflection. Through all these hands the Tarot has passed, gathering meaning, accumulating the hopes and wishes of those who use it, triggering the imagination, and acting as a pathway to unseen worlds.

PERSONAL EVOLUTION WITH TAROT

This kind of process may be mirrored to some degree in your own use of Tarot, in that it will evolve and be shaped by your own life experiences. Your personal relationship with the cards may be modified over the years. My first encounter, as I've described, was with the Rider-Waite pack, a vividly-colored and fully pictorial set of suits and Trumps all heavily imbued with esoteric symbolism. I marveled at it, was transported by it even. However, after a period of research and decades of using Tarot cards, this has evolved into a quieter sense of affection and respect for that particular pack, while on the other hand my interest in the symbolism of the Major Arcana of the Marseilles pack has grown and proved to be a more lasting flame. This is my Tarot of choice, and it is the version I feature in this book. It is the closest representation we have of the core of the Tarot tradition, and for this reason it remains a classic and, to my mind, offers the best way to try to understand the essence of Tarot.

Choosing Your Pack

There is not one single "true" Tarot pack because of the variations in traditional designs of the Triumphs and the branching lines of transmission into different countries and cultures. This may indeed be a good thing; the Tarot's own "triumph" is that the archetypal images on the cards are so strong that the actual designs can take a modicum of variation and still retain their magnetism. Anything genuinely mythical has the capacity to appear in a range of representations: there are many differing images of the Holy Grail or the Green Man, for instance. A good divinatory system has room for adaptation; one where every detail is legislated quickly becomes dated and rigid.[2] It is fascinating to compare these differing Tarot designs and to pick out variations in detail, but more as a way of enhancing our understanding and confirming the real essence of the card, rather than pointing the way to a "correct" version of Tarot.

But to follow the guidelines and interpretations in this book, I recommend that you buy a Marseilles-style pack. The one most commonly available was originally marketed by B. P. Grimaud, a French playing-card manufacturer. This pack was republished around 1969 and is still widely sold in various editions, though Grimaud is now subsumed into the company France Cartes, or France Cards. One of their decks, called the Ancien Tarot de Marseille, is a reproduction of an eighteenth-century pack with some adjustment from the Grimaud artists and a resulting color scheme that is predominantly blue, red, and yellow. It is a good standard version of Marseilles Tarot, but any Marseilles Tarot pack should do fine for our purposes. US Games also makes a couple of good decks. If you cannot find a deck in a bookstore or gift store, then try online sellers. Amazon's French site (*www.amazon.fr*) is a particularly good source because of the long-standing publication of traditional Tarot packs in France.

I suggest that you choose a straightforward Marseilles set of cards, not one where the High Priestess and the Pope are replaced by Juno and Jupiter, a pack often known as Tarot de Besançon; these look out of place among the other Trumps, especially for divinatory purposes.

It's advisable to make one pack of cards your prime choice for use; you'll build up a rapport with it, and you'll find it easier to interpret layouts this way. However, many of us love collecting Tarot cards, or comparing versions, so you may quickly be tempted to acquire other types of packs. And as you progress with Tarot, you may find, as I did, that your affinity changes somewhat.

Here is how my own Tarot collection and my relationship with the Tarot progressed. After I had bought my first two packs, the Marseilles and the Rider-Waite Tarots, I went on the hunt for more. Over the next few years, general interest in Tarot blossomed, and more packs were beginning to appear in the shops. Living in London in the early seventies, I haunted Watkins Books, long a home of esoteric books and now of Tarot cards too. I bought practically every pack I could find with the idea of forming a collection. The choice was still very limited though; I acquired a Swiss Besançon pack, the Richard Gardner/Insight Institute pack (a hybrid of Rider-Waite and Marseilles), and a gilded version of the Oswald Wirth pack. I bought other Tarots that were too fanciful for use, and some double-ended packs that were really just for card games. It wasn't long before my collection, now into double digits, divided itself clearly between packs I could use for Tarot study and divination and those that were just curiosities. As the world began to take up Tarot, I found the proliferation, quite frankly, bewildering, and I decided to limit my collection and enjoy what I had there already. However, I did make occasional additions; a special find in Venice were two beautiful reproductions of historic Tarocchi packs. By this time I had decided to limit my interests mainly to traditional Tarot. Here, I felt, lay the true story.

Lately, for the purposes of researching this book (or so I tell myself), I have bought more packs from the much wider selection of traditional Tarot now available. The Golden Tarot, for instance, is a gorgeous historical reproduction of the fifteenth-century Visconti-Sforza pack, with sensitive restorations of three missing cards. Reproductions of key Marseilles packs, such as the 1701 Madénie and the 1761 Conver Tarots, are also valued acquisitions to my collection.[3] But for the purposes of historical study and comparing packs, there is now a wealth of digital imagery available online. The British Museum collection online is an excellent place to start, via a search for Tarot cards in its vast digital photo library. Images can also be emailed to you without charge if they are purely for private study.[4] I love to lose myself in the images of historic Tarot packs that I've downloaded and printed out. The only cost, although admittedly not cheap, is that of the printing ink.

But you do not have to take up card collecting or be a Tarot historian; acquiring just one Tarot deck for your use is the main thing here. My advice is to start with the most traditional style of Marseilles pack that you can get hold of, and branch out from there if you wish. But keep the Marseilles Triumphs at the center of your Tarot practice if you plan to follow the sequence in this book.

Keeping Your Cards

How you store your Tarot cards is a matter of personal preference. Some people like to wrap the deck in silk (black silk is said to preserve their energies best). Others might consider it enough to put them back in the cardboard case in which they are sold, or even just cheerfully put a rubber band around them and drop them back in the drawer! Long ago, I had a Tarot box made for me in Morocco out of cedar wood, crafted to my design with Tarot symbols inlaid on the lid. I recall watching the craftsman cut slivers off an old tin can to make the silver decorations! I still have it, and use it, but I don't consider it essential. I do like to house my Tarot carefully and with respect, but I believe that the important thing is to build up a relationship with the cards, and with one or two packs in particular. The way you keep them is really up to you.

USING THE TAROT TRIUMPHS

As explained earlier, only the twenty-two Tarot Trumps of the Major Arcana are used in this book. Any references from now on to "the pack" will refer to the Triumphs, unless specifically indicated otherwise. You may wish to extend your Tarot readings later to include the four suits, but even so, working first with the Trumps will give you a good basis for this. Like many other Tarot practitioners, I prefer to just use the twenty-two Trumps. As I have found, and the Fool's Mirror layout proves in chapter seven, it is not essential to bring in the four suits at all. The Triumphs stand as a viable set in their own right; they have an independent existence and were not generated along with the four-suit playing-card pack. The suits are based more on numerical values and court cards; their interpretation tends to be more dependent on pre-formulated attributions, which can lead to a shallower kind of divination. I am not saying that the four suits cannot be interpreted with a genuine degree of significance, but it is hard to do this without a thorough study of the meaning of number and its possibilities for interpretation. Nearly all Tarot practitioners would, in any case, agree that the Tarot Trumps have more power and weight in a reading than the cards of the suits, even when those suits are also represented as images, as in the case of the Rider-Waite pack.

Keynote Interpretations of the Tarot Trumps

What follows are brief keynote summaries of the twenty-two Triumphs, which serve as a foundation for interpreting the cards in a simple divination layout. This is something we will tackle in chapter four, so the idea here is to give the basis needed for considering the cards in combination, applying them to a real-life question or situation.

I have given these more as brief portraits of the images and what they represent as archetypes; it is important to make a connection with the kind of living presence of each card rather than with just a string of attributes. But I've also shown how archetype and attribute can connect—an important bridge to cross in Tarot practice. Becoming fluent in seeing how archetypal qualities may manifest in everyday human concerns is the essential skill that a Tarot reader needs to develop.

Accompanying these interpretations, you will find thumbnail line-drawn images of each card. These are intended for immediate guidance and are based on traditional images from the Marseilles packs. They are drawn by Robert Lee-Wade; we have conferred as to which details to include so as to give a generic version of the pack with appropriate, but not definitive, detail.[5] The full-size drawings of each card appear in chapter five.

These keynote interpretations may remain useful even after you have graduated to more complex readings. It is often helpful to be able to come back and refresh our minds with the simpler attributions.

You may also like to make a list of keywords associated with each card, both to clarify your understanding and for future reference. For this, I suggest that you take one card at a time, read the interpretation below, look at the image, and jot down just a few attributions. Don't spend too much time on this, because you will come to the deeper interpretations later in the book; save your main efforts for that.

0. The Fool

The Fool represents the beginning and the end of the journey. The Fool may know everything, or nothing. He tends to live in a blissful state of ignorance. Optimism, blind faith, open-mindedness, innocence, adventurousness, and naivety are the Fool's characteristics. Folly is a part of life. His attributes are travel, poverty, ridicule, the outsider, and youthfulness. He is the wild card and the human quest.

1. The Magician

The Magician is the master of magic and illusion. Using the four elements of earth, water, fire, and air, represented here by the pentacle, cup, knife, and wand, he conjures up the ever-changing forms of life in colorful variety. In person, he may be deceitful, clever, creative, and charismatic. His attributes are inspiration, confidence, magic, gambling, wit, and spontaneity.

2. The High Priestess

The High Priestess is privy to the wisdom of the temple. She imparts this to those who have ears to hear or eyes to read the words of her book. Her way is contemplative, retiring, patient, and intuitive. In her presence these are appropriate: divination, meditation, learning, reading, counseling, and silence. Questions can be more important than answers.

3. The Empress

The Empress rules her domain confidently, in possession of her full powers. She epitomizes female sexuality and authority, and she protects the weak while remaining strong in her position. She represents the law of the land, fruitfulness, feminine power, capricious command, and righteous certainty. Her badges of office also represent formality and the fixed order. But she has her own secrets, too, and she may be pregnant with a new heir.

4. The Emperor

The Emperor's profile is fit for minting on a copper coin. He is seen as the ruler, one who keeps the boundaries but who may also block the way. His command is strong. He represents hierarchy, steady will, and reliability. He is the ultimate figure of male authority, acting as father, leader, and the upholder of honor. He controls money, economy, and policy.

5. The Pope

The Pope connects the human and spiritual worlds. He can be a teacher, a priest, and a benefactor, sustaining transcendent values. He represents blessing, forgiveness, and conscience, but also potential loss of individuality and forced submission. Teaching, religion, confession, and interpretation come under his sway. He operates from tradition rather than personal power. The Pope can be an emblem of wise teaching or of dogmatic views.

6. The Lover

The Lover must choose; desire arises naturally, but heart and head are both involved. The hand strays one way, the eye another. Love comes with responsibility, and at a price. Whatever is chosen, consequences will ensue. Passion, love, and union are all possible here; so are misery and regret. Relationships are just one interpretation of this image, which can also represent a serious decision to be made, perhaps with moral implications.

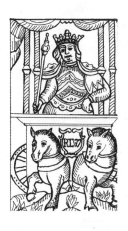

7. The Chariot

The Chariot is one entity, composed of charioteer, horses, and a wheeled carriage. Together, they represent a winning combination and can indicate moving forward with a project or journey. The use of skill, the harnessing of energy, and the choice of a suitable vehicle are all important to make that combination work. But caution is also implied; the charioteer must be ever vigilant so that his horses don't part company or his vehicle doesn't overturn at speed. Ambition, drive, and travel are shown here.

8. Justice

Justice, clear-sighted, witnesses every action and its corresponding consequences. She offers more than the law of action and reaction: she brings fairness, truth, and a way to right wrongs. Judgment, punishment, and redress are associated with Justice, but so are mercy and understanding. Justice represents the struggle for balance and perfection, and the need for compromise.

9. The Hermit

The Hermit follows his own path, but in accordance with values of a higher order. He is solitary, but he may impart his knowledge to someone who truly seeks it. The Hermit represents individuality, patience, frugality, and steadfastness. He can also signify poverty or making do with very little. Aloneness, but not necessarily loneliness, is a keynote here.

10. The Wheel of Fortune

The Wheel will never stop turning. Hope and ambition flourish on the way up; disappointment may follow on the way down. The Wheel of Fortune can be a rapid path to success, or a treadmill, or an unexpected turn of luck for good or ill. Chance affects everyone. Acceptance of change and taking opportunities as they are presented are potential benefits.

11. Strength

Strength tames through quiet confidence. She knows when to apply pressure and when to let go, using minimum force to achieve the best result. Powers of female influence and gentle persuasion are implied, and ways of mastering aggression. Both submission and dominance may show themselves here in questions of gain and loss, gentleness, and superiority.

12. The Hanged Man

The Hanged Man has turned his world upside-down, and he delights in this fresh view. Playfulness and poise are indicated. So are loss of status, stripping of authority, and reversal of intentions. The meaning is in all these aspects: inversion, vision, sacrifice, revelation, cleverness, balance, and the need to understand matters from a different perspective.

13. Death

Death swings his sickle, his profile etched sharply; he is a fearful presence. He comes with inevitability, and he brooks no opposition. But he is also a part of life. There is new growth; hands and faces pushing up through the earth look bright and serene. This is the card of endings and beginnings. It may be time to make a clean sweep.

14. Temperance

Temperance symbolizes generosity and compassion. She is moderation, too, in the sense that when the water of life is always at your disposal, you do not need to drink it too greedily. Calm confidence, a measured approach, and graceful movement are her watchwords. Regeneration, renewable resources, and equal opportunities are some of her modern attributes.

15. The Devil

The Devil binds us because there is a price that must be paid for everything. The fear of what he represents may shrink away, though, if we confront it, or if we are willing to shoulder an unwelcome burden. Humor is an ally; the Devil is a grotesque caricature of life and must not be given too much power.

16. The Tower

The Tower shows that the higher you build, the farther there is to fall. Pride and ambition have their limitations. But with destruction, liberation can come. The Tower can be a loss of prestige, confidence, or self-esteem, and in a material sense, a loss of money, home, or worldly goods. However, it can also be an escape from prison, a welcome shock.

17. The Star

The Star is naked, unlike Temperance, and her jugs decant, rather than pouring from one to the other. This is release, with no pretense or elaboration. Healing, generosity, and sincerity prevail. But the stars and the bird denote more: a journey to the celestial spheres, a message or messenger, and perhaps a mission to rescue something precious.

18. The Moon

The Moon looks down on an eerie landscape, where reality and dream overlap. This is a world of illusions, but it can also denote imagination and inspiration. The Moon governs secrets and fantasies. It rules empathy and psychic powers, but also distortion, deceit, and false images. Tread carefully when there is only the moon to light the way.

19. The Sun

The Sun represents truth, warmth, and common sense. It can also signify riches and the natural goodness of everyday life. There is a lack of pretense under the rays of the sun, which give us the confidence to be honest and open. The Sun's rays restore energy, and its image represents good nature, cheerfulness, and simplicity.

20. Judgment

Judgment arrives with the sound of the trumpet. It can be a sudden call to arouse us, a harbinger of a fundamental change. The moment of awakening comes loud and clear. Former habits and attire are lost, and there must be a completely new start. Beginnings, exposure, or a summons out of the blue are attributes of the card.

21. The World

The World represents completion and fulfillment. It denotes a combination of energy and stability, or of motion and fixity. It could show the welcome conclusion to a matter, a chance to rest for a while within the daily turning of the wheel. But then again, it could be a situation that has persisted for a long time and is about to change. It might represent tedious effort or a joyous dance of life.

TRIADS AND THREES

Appropriately enough, for chapter three, I'd like to introduce the significance of the number three in relation to the Tarot. The sequence of the twenty-two Tarot Trumps lends itself well to considering numerical values, and straightaway it's obvious that the twenty-one numbered cards divide up into three sets of seven.[6] Three is therefore a good place to start exploring the numbering. "Three-ness" may be less prominent in Tarot than, say, its sevenfold structure, which we shall come to later, or its interesting juxtaposition of twenty-one and twenty-two; but the pattern of three is, in my view, more useful in learning the process of Tarot divination. It opens up the idea of three as the prime basis for the creative forces of the universe, the three elements that lie behind any situation in human life, and it also gives us a base from which to explore the interactive possibilities of the cards.

Three forces, or a trinity, are said to represent the basic dynamic of the universe, an idea that is found almost universally in various cosmologies and spiritual traditions. Taking a lead from the kabbalistic Tree of Life and the teachings of G. I. Gurdjieff, these can broadly be defined as the active, the passive, and the reconciling forces. The active force is outgoing, often creative, and expansive. The passive force is negative, or resisting; it receives the active force and contains or controls it. The reconciling, or uniting, force, sometimes equated with consciousness itself, balances out the opposing nature of the other two forces and may produce something new from them.

Although this concept of three forces may at first seem very abstract, with a little thought it is in fact easy to find everyday examples of their interplay at work. For instance: I have a good idea. It hits me suddenly, and I know it's wonderful, that I can do it, and that everyone will love it. But after sleeping on it, I am assailed by doubt. *What if it doesn't go to plan? Have I really got the time and energy to commit to it? No, I was wrong—it's definitely a bad idea!* But give it a little more time, and on day three I may well think, *Yes, I can do it after all, but I need to do it like this, not that.* I've processed the objections, modified the format, and found ways to make it viable. It is no longer a blissfully creative impulse, nor a dark denying response, but something with practical validity that I will have to work on further to put into action. I cannot do it automatically, and so my conscious participation, the reconciling force, is needed to realize it. Does this sound familiar? Whether it's throwing a party or writing a three-volume memoir, you will probably find that your splendid creative idea has to go through these successive stages.

Let's see how this law of three can be applied to the principles of Tarot.

1. Three engenders and forms a relationship. Every Tarot card reading involves three elements: the cards, the diviner undertaking the reading, and the question or person inquiring of the cards. This triad of divination allows energy to circulate and an interpretation to arise. It also shows why it may be very difficult to read the cards for yourself, since the question/questioner has to be a separate factor from the diviner; to make that work, you have to place the question, in some sense, outside your own personal feelings and responses.

2. Three-ness can be found at work within the individual cards by looking for two opposing forces, or contradictions, and then figuring out what they might signify, or what might reconcile them. For instance, Temperance shows water flowing in two directions at once. How can these two streams be part of the same thing? The answer might lie in seeing them the way opposing energies can be balanced to produce harmony, and as an emblem of how resources are renewed on a greater scale. Studying each card in this way can be enlightening.

3. Three makes a situation. If you take three Tarot cards, either for study or for a reading, you have the essence of a situation with a dynamic. One card simply is;

two cards either oppose or unite with each other; but three cards give insight into the unique mix and interplay of a situation.

WORKING WITH THREES

Let's start with number three of the three propositions about "three-ness."

Once you have become familiar with the basic ways of interpreting the cards (in this case, the keynotes just given), you can start to see how they work in combination. This is the main basis of Tarot divination, and it takes pride of place in the Fool's Mirror layout. I hope this will become clearer over the next few chapters, where the relating of the cards to each other gives the reading its individuality and relevance.

For now, I suggest that you pick trios of cards, preferably at random, and try to see how they interact with one another. In the next chapter, you will be encouraged to do this as a divination practice—that is, in answer to a question; but here the aim is to make free combinations of the cards and observe their mutual influence.

Here's an example undertaken specifically for this book. It is done as an exercise in studying three cards together, but not in relation to a real question.

I shuffle the cards, then hold them facedown with one hand and pick out three cards with the other. If you choose to do the same, it really doesn't matter how you pick out the cards, as long as you can't see which ones you're choosing. (The exercise usually works better if you give yourself a surprise.)

I turn over the Magician, the Devil, and the Emperor.

First, I take note of my reactions. The Magician appeals to me. I do not like the Devil (who does?), but I must accept his right to be here. The aim in the Fool's Mirror system of Tarot is to accept the validity of all the cards and understand the rightful place they have in the pack. The Emperor looks very severe and has a degree of impenetrability. Having noted my reactions, I now want to go beyond them, to see their energies at work with each other, so I employ a few questions to help me:

1. *What similarities are there between the cards?* This will help me to perceive the nature of this particular interaction. Briefly, I would say: maleness, authority, cleverness, and potential trickery.

2. *What differences are there?* One figure represents creative freedom, one is shackled, and one has authority. There are many more differences that you might choose to respond to; we will never see a spread exactly the same way twice, but that is also indicative of the richness of the Tarot Triumph symbols.

3. *What positives and negatives can be perceived?* Another way of putting this question might be, How might the cards work together as a team? My answer is: Strong on willpower, ingenuity, and assertion. But together, they could also be unpleasant, arrogant, and deceitful.

4. *What happens if the cards are seen in a sequence?* I look at them in the order that they turned up and see what story they tell: The Magician meets an almost impossible obstacle and manages to overcome it by great skill and his magical powers. He is elevated to a position of high status as a result. But in his new role, he now has to take more responsibility and has less freedom.

I've recounted that in a "mythic" way, but of course it could just as well be interpreted as a challenge encountered in modern-day business or a crisis in a personal relationship. I would probably want to vary the words I've used, and the type of outcome, but the essence of the story would be the same. You can also try changing the order of the cards and seeing what difference it makes. There are six possible orders, and each can suggest a different storyline. What are these six possible stories?

5. *What stories or myths do the three cards remind you of?* Once you've looked at the combination of the cards from different angles, you can ask what associations they bring up. My main story is "A Rainbow in Silk," a story from Central Asia that I have retold in one of my children's books. It concerns an elderly courtier who is asked by the king on pain of death to create something novel to amuse His Majesty. Finally, as the courtier is about to be executed for failing in his task, he sees a rainbow through the tears that have formed in his eyes and is inspired to create "rainbow silk," a textile that is still worn in Uzbekistan today.[7]

Next, I think of "The Sorcerer's Apprentice," a poem written by Goethe that I used to listen to in a musical version as a child.[8] Here, the magician's apprentice is asked to fetch water while the sorcerer is off on a break. The apprentice decides to cast a spell to get the spirits to perform the chores, but his inadequate training means that he can't then stop the magic from working and the room flooding! His master returns in time to prevent total disaster.

There is much to ponder in these two stories, including questions of vanity, creativity, and responsibility.

6. *What lessons and truths emerge?* I can see from the way the cards seem to respond to one another that

magic cannot be commanded by authority or be used for a dubious building of power without adverse results. Creativity must have a degree of freedom.

From these questions, you can see how a short foray into contemplating just three of the Tarot cards provides a colorful, varied, and detailed view of how they can interact. Three isn't said to be the creative number of the universe for nothing. I suggest that you try the same process. You can vary the order of the questions if you need to, though it's easier to start off with similarities and differences to get a handle on the lineup of cards.

In the next chapter, you can build on this work by learning the three-card reading.

STAYING SAFE WITH TAROT

Using the cards in this more considered but fluid way is a good counterbalance to the risk of getting overwhelmed by their powerful imagery. Tarot images can certainly strike a chord in the imagination that resonates with deep forces, memories, and images in our own psyche. My advice is neither to try to prevent this from happening, nor to try to force it to happen, either of which could be unsettling. Instead, be cautious and apply a gentle but persistent discipline.

Suggested guidelines are:

+ Work with Tarot for a limited time each day. One or two hours is usually sufficient.

+ Put your cards away when you have finished using them.

+ Clear your head afterward, preferably by engaging in some physical activity, such as going for a walk.

* Do not jump to conclusions about what the cards "mean." By all means, allow your intuition to work; but consider any "messages" or strong insights as interesting rather than authoritative.

* Build up your knowledge and practice of Tarot steadily. This will provide you with a good foundation.

TAROT AND DREAMS

You might also like to note your dreams while you are engaged with the Tarot, as they may relate in some way to the work that you're doing with the cards, or have a different quality to them, perhaps containing striking imagery.[9] Just before I started to write this book, for instance, and I was still in the mulling stage, I had a vivid dream about a talking black bird, which hopped onto my finger. I did not attempt to pin the image down too closely, but I was delighted, and I left with the hope that the book might "speak" to readers, or indeed that Tarot might speak to me further while I was engaged in the writing process. If you write down your own dreams and look back at what you've written later on, you may see some interesting correspondences with using Tarot cards. But if the dreams become too intense or unsettling in some way, have a break from the cards for a few days. It may be a sign that you are getting too involved in their imagery, or perhaps that the process of acquainting yourself with the cards needs extra time to find its own level in your psyche.

I do not recommend trying to take Tarot into your dreams at this stage, for instance by keeping a card under your pillow. In other words, don't force: just allow.

MEDITATION, NOT VISUALIZATION

If you have a meditation practice, keep it up when you are studying the Tarot. It helps to center, calm, and free you. And by this, I mean a simple core meditation practice, one that relies on mindfulness, or observing breath, or listening to a sound. This is true meditation, rather than visualizations that encourage a flow of imagery. Strictly speaking, visualizations are not meditations at all. If you want to encourage Tarot to work at a deep level in your imagination, I suggest that you not do any other visualizations while you are still in the developmental phase of absorbing the imagery of the cards.

KEEPING IT SIMPLE—AND POWERFUL

If you are new to the Tarot, I recommend that you make your first task that of getting to know the basic images, the names and numbering of the cards, and their keynote meanings. By all means, look at variations of the Marseilles pack; but keep in mind that differing details may have crept in by accident, as different generations of card makers produced their own designs. You can either concentrate on familiarizing yourself with just one pack, or acquaint yourself with some idea of what the variations might be, while keeping the main "blueprint" in mind.

I also recommend studying Tarot as a self-contained system, rather than trying to work out straightaway how it might correspond to astrology, Kabbalah, Christianity, or any other framework. Once you have acquired facility with the cards, and are confident of knowing the system, then it's fine to consider other attributions.[10]

Now, we enter the age-old tradition of fortune-telling.

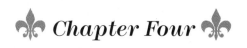

Chapter Four

THE WANDERING FORTUNE-TELLER

The scene is a marketplace in Northern Italy. It's in a small seaside town and has just a few canopied stalls set out, serving locals and holidaymakers alike. The year is 1972. I scan the stalls, and my eye is caught by an old lady standing erect behind her table, her hands busy spreading out a pack of Tarot cards. I can see that they are a local type known as Tarocchi in these parts, brightly colored and a little smaller than the cards I am used to.

As I glance in the woman's direction, a young couple approaches her. I can't speak Italian at this early stage in my life so I have to interpret what's happening through their looks and gestures. The pair are clearly in love, and the young woman appears to be asking for a Tarot reading. The old lady gazes at her, then her brown, weather-worn face creases into a welcoming smile.

I try to observe what is happening at a safe distance as market shoppers come and go. I'm fascinated, but don't want to look as though I'm intruding. The next thing I can see is that all the cards—the full pack of seventy-eight, which includes the four suits—are spread out right across the table, most of them faceup. It looks like a random spread, lacking in pattern or layout to me, but it can't be, because the old lady points to this card and then that, talking to the couple. Although her reading is for the girl, she politely includes the man in the interaction. She speaks gently, but with confidence, and there is a lilt, an expressiveness in her voice as she tells the story of what she sees in the cards. The young woman and her boyfriend nod. As the reading draws to a close, I see the fortune-teller smile warmly, benignly, and spread out her hands as though she is saying, "This is the tale the cards tell. This is what I can convey to you. Don't be afraid—life is unfolding for you, and you have nothing to fear." It is a moment of compassionate inclusion.

Who was the old lady? I have thought about her many times since. I can only speculate, as I relish the impact of the experience, which is still vivid in my mind. But I would guess that she was from a long line of fortune-tellers, those who had passed on the meaning of the Tarot cards through centuries of divination. This is all the more likely because the encounter occurred in the part of Italy where Tarot itself took root and evolved in the fifteenth and sixteenth centuries. Perhaps she was one of the last of her kind to practice the traditional form of Tarot fortune-telling, going from house to house, or standing, as she did, in marketplaces and at fairs and festivals. Although today you can easily find a Tarot reader, finding someone who has been taught Tarot as part of a way of life, through an oral tradition, is a rarity.

I feel lucky to have witnessed this, and I draw on it now to illustrate what practical, traditional fortune-telling with the Tarot may be like at its best. It shows us how a reading can be set up, very simply and even in public if need be, to give an answer to a question in a relatively short space of time. The Tarot reader here was receptive to the cards and her clients, and there was nothing hard or mercenary about her manner. It was, to my eyes, genuine divination rather than a mechanical, rote reading, and yet it needed to deliver; the old lady did the job that she was asked to do, giving an answer to the question as best she could, and concluding the transaction with goodwill.

It's important to keep this basic premise in mind and see the fundamental practicalities of Tarot reading as a foundation for our own forays into divination. We may study the deeper meanings, long history, and subtle nuances of the Tarot, but if we are going to give readings, the ultimate premise is that of question and answer. So, in this chapter, I invite you to begin as "fortune-teller," to consult the cards and obtain a reading in a similarly direct and simple way.

PREPARING FOR YOUR FIRST READING

Our first reading will use just three cards, after a look at the preliminaries of setting up a Tarot reading.

Familiarizing Yourself with the Cards

It's important to become familiar with the names and images of each card before trying out a Tarot divination. If they are new to you, I suggest that you get to know them all as if you were becoming acquainted with guests at a dinner party, or fellow travelers on an expedition. You don't need to know everything about the Tarot Triumphs at this stage, but it's crucial to be able to recognize all of them and have a sense of their key meanings. That way, your intuition can work with the card combinations because you have already absorbed the essential identity of the individual cards. You can use the illustrations in this book, your own pack, and the two sets of descriptions that I've given earlier to get to know the twenty-two cards. It's good to master the numbering too if you can, but it's not compulsory at this point. We'll discuss the sequence of the numbers in the next chapter.

Framing the Question

What follows is general advice that is useful to have at the start, even if you do not need to implement it all straightaway.

Every divination reading is based around a question. It can be very specific, such as "Will I get the job?" or it could relate to a general situation, such as "Where am I at this point in my life?" But remember that a question always lies at the heart of the reading. If you are divining for someone else—which will probably be the case more often than not—you need to ask that person to define the question. There are a couple of choices to make here:

1. Find out if the person (referred to as the *querent* from here on) has a particular question they wish to ask, or if they want to make a general inquiry about their current situation.

2. If it's a specific question, for preference, ask them to state it aloud. If this is not appropriate, then request that they formulate it clearly in thought, and hold it in mind.

For readings that use just a few cards, such as the one we are about to explore, it is more straightforward to know what question is being asked. If that's not possible, then working without knowing what the question is can certainly be a little scary. On the other hand, it frees you up to talk about the way you see the reading. Sometimes, even if you have been told the question, you may find that this is not the real issue, and that one question may conceal another. It's not uncommon for the querent to say after the reading something like, "You know, I wanted to know about my work, but in fact you've reached the heart of the matter, which was really about my relationship. I can see that now."

The Significator

In most Tarot layouts there is a *significator*, a card selected to stand on its own, which indicates the querent at the present time, or the topic of the question asked. Although the three-card reading I'm about to explain does not include a significator, we will come to it directly afterward with a four-card layout. It's also worth mentioning now because it is relevant to the issue of whether the diviner is told the question or not; if there is a significator in the layout, even if the querent doesn't voice the question aloud, the significator will usually give you a handle on the situation. So, for most Tarot readings, the significator is a signpost that you can use to point the way to the nature of the situation.

Reading for Others

It is always up to you whether you agree to read the Tarot for another person or not. We'll investigate the ethics and safe practices of divination more fully in chapter eight, but right at the start here, it's a good basic premise on which to found your practice.

If you have an uneasy feeling about doing a reading for someone, or if they try to pressure you, my advice is to withdraw as gracefully and tactfully as you can. You can always say that your mind isn't clear enough after all and suggest that they come back to you in a few weeks' time.

When you are learning Tarot, it's very possible that you'll ask friends or people you know if they would like to have their cards read. As time goes on, it's often better to wait until you're asked, but of course at the start no one will know that you're available to do this unless you tell them! And actively offering your services (at the beginning, definitely not for money[1]) can be a useful way of screening out individuals for whom you don't feel ready or willing to read the cards. You can also phrase your invitation in such a way that you can tackle the kind of reading you feel most confident with, for instance by saying "I'm just getting into practice with this, and I'd like to suggest a general reading as to where things stand at present, if that's OK." Or "Could you make it a question that is about something specific, but nothing too important to you?" This way, you are not dealing with life-or-death situations or opening a can of worms by venturing into very sensitive territory.

Reading for Yourself

Since Tarot is a fluid, imaginative medium of divination, it is best used, in my view, to give readings for others. However, when you are first learning to work with the cards, you may need to use yourself for practice. In this case, I suggest picking a question where the issue is a minor one, a matter of harmless interest, or even about a situation completely outside your own affairs. "Why is she being so difficult at the moment?" might pinpoint the passing trouble with a friend who isn't her usual self. "What kind of holiday should I take?" could give you some useful ideas for your next vacation. You could even have fun trying to figure out who will win the next election.

A word of caution, though: When I was getting acquainted with another form of card divination (later to become known as the Tree of Life Oracle, for which I wrote the handbook[2]), I decided to ask who would win the Grand National, the biggest horse race in the British calendar. I am not a betting person, but I thought it would be fun to have a go. I did a three-card reading, and two of the cards that turned up were called the Man of Blood and the Drunkard. I checked the list of runners. Aha! Red Rum was an outsider in the race—surely he would fit the cards rather well? I put some money on him. He won! (And, incidentally, he went on to become one of the most renowned racehorses in history.) Next year, a little guiltily, I confess, I tried the same thing. It didn't work and I lost my money. The next and final year, I did the same, and lost yet again. The money lost just about canceled out money won.

I had learned my lesson. There *is* such a thing as beginner's luck; there *is* such a thing as "the innocent Fool," who looks in the Fool's Mirror and can sometimes get away with a great deal. As it is said, "Fools rush in where angels fear to tread."[3] But once you are no longer innocent, no longer a child in such matters, you need to proceed with respect and ethical consideration at the forefront; otherwise the gods will surely take away what they have granted. And if you use divination to serve as a form of gambling—Tarot divination and gambling have certainly co-existed in their historical forms—then your prowess at reading the Tarot may be reduced to a basic, materialistic level. I was lucky in another way that I didn't win again. It could well have coarsened my sensitivity to the cards.

First Approaches

To sum up, first attempts at Tarot reading are often best kept as light, playful, and varied. Take opportunities that come your way, give it your best shot, and don't worry too much if you can't always fathom whether the reading is a "success." Sometimes we may miss the mark. Sometimes the person asking the question blocks the reading with resistance or an adverse emotional attitude. But sometimes, too, the reading may be more relevant than is obvious at the time. The querent might ask you about one matter, but you could feel the need to respond with something different. Later, the querent may say, "You know, what you said turned out to be right on the mark. I didn't realize it at the time." With Tarot divination, we need to go with what the cards tells us.

It's important not to let our own preconceptions get in the way either. I once read a horoscope for a girl I employed in my business. It seemed to point to a kind of violence in her nature, at the least an aggressive streak, but I'd never seen any evidence of that and I didn't quite have the confidence to mention it. I was running a vintage clothes shop at the time and she was my chief assistant, so her behavior did matter to me. A few weeks later, I asked her about an awkward acquaintance who hung around our shop and wouldn't leave. I noticed that all of a sudden, he had disappeared. "I took the broomstick to him," she told me proudly. "Drove him out. Don't think he'll be back anytime soon." My mouth fell open as I silently reckoned that the horoscope had been right after all.

Casebook and Notes

Should you keep a casebook, or notes of some form, of your Tarot readings and your experiences of divination? This is up to you. I didn't keep such a record and think it would certainly be interesting now to look back over it and remind myself of readings and Tarot forays I no longer recall. A colleague has a record of all his consultations with the I-Ching stretching back more than fifty years, which is a fascinating document that he permitted me to read.

However, Tarot is different from the I-Ching. Tarot relies on a blend of knowledge and intuition or imagination, and a Tarot reading is very much a response to a particular question asked at a particular time, so a casebook can't act as a source of fixed interpretations. In one reading, for instance, the Emperor might stand for a father figure; in another reading, it might stand for individual willpower. So, if you do keep notes, use them primarily to recall your response to the way the cards developed on each occasion, and how the reading went overall. You could also perhaps compare the range of possible meanings that a particular card revealed in a number of readings. Notebooks can be useful adjuncts to developing your relationship with Tarot, but treat them as interesting records rather than a kind of bible that you consult for interpreting future readings.

THE THREE-CARD READING

The three-card reading is a simple but effective way of reading the Tarot. Although it's a good place to start if you are a novice, it is also a useful method for any Tarot reader to give a snapshot reading for an individual, or if you want to obtain a quick take on a situation.

Naming the Question

Ask the individual (the querent) to phrase a simple question about what they would like to know and to tell you what it is. You can explain that this is a brief reading, and the question is best applied to a specific and simple issue. Alternatively, the reading could provide a snapshot view of the querent's situation at present. The querent should say which reading they would prefer.

For Tarot readings in general, where the querent identifies the question, try to encourage this to be spoken in a succinct manner. "Where is my relationship going?" is more appropriate than a long explanation of all the factors, emotions, and doubts involved. Too much detail can cloud the reading and subtly invite bias to enter the diviner's mind. Of course, for a three-card reading such as this, for a simple or minor query, it would be completely out of proportion anyway to give the full background to a question. But it will become important as the number of cards used increases and the complexity of the spread develops. So it is worth making the point right at the start and getting into practice for this by encouraging the querent to frame up the question clearly in a few words.

Method

Shuffle the cards thoroughly, making sure that they are all the right way up and that they are facedown during the shuffling. Spread them out either in your hands or on a convenient surface, and ask the querent to pick out three cards. He or she should hand each one to you as it is chosen. Neither of you should look at the cards until all three have been selected. Then you, as the reader, should turn the cards over and let them be seen. For this form of Tarot reading, the order they are drawn in doesn't matter.

Then, bearing the question in mind, study the cards and see what the combination of the three brings to your mind. Speak when you're ready. This is where you really take the plunge! Remember that it's the connection between you, the querent, and the cards that generates the reading. Use your knowledge of Tarot as a foundation;

try to put preexisting judgments about the person out of your mind, and allow the story to surface. Note that we haven't set up any time parameters, so you are looking at the triad of cards as an entity, rather than seeing them as past, present, or future. (We will come to that shortly, both later in this chapter and in chapter six.) It's fine to ask a question or two if you need to. For instance, if the Chariot turns up, you might want to find out if the person has any travel plans in mind, since not every appearance of the Chariot will indicate travel, even though it can be one strong association with that card.

This is a quick reading, and a few minutes should be enough to share what you see with the querent. I recommend keeping it to a short exchange, with no more than a little conversation. Don't be tempted to elaborate, to say more than you can quickly or easily see in the combination of cards. Otherwise, too much imagination can come in, and it's possible to drift off on one's own chain of association. And if you really can't see anything, and can't make sense of the triad of cards, be brave enough to say so! If you've kept the whole setup light, then the other person won't mind too much. You can offer to try again another day.

I sprang into action at a party once as a wandering fortune-teller. I decided to take a pack of Tarot cards with me and offer to read them if any of the guests showed an interest. I stuck the pack rather theatrically into a red sash that I was wearing, and I pulled them out on request. I did this while in circulation—no props, fancy seating arrangements, or calls for silence. It was all done within the merry chatter around me. One of the guests was a young woman who was planning to work as an au pair in America for the summer. I can't recall the exact cards, but I do remember saying to her, "I think you'll be doing a lot more traveling than you expect." She shook her head and said she'd be staying put in the one location the whole time. I thought that perhaps I had it wrong. But when I next caught up with her, after the summer, she said that the job had been awful so she'd quit and spent the rest of her time traveling. One point on this example: ideally, neither accept nor reject the other person's immediate take on the reading that you give. You have said your piece; leave it to work in its own way.

It's possible to do a three-card reading for yourself, if you wish, keeping in mind the cautionary recommendations I've made earlier. Do it for something self-contained and not too important. For example, today my husband and I have decided to walk in a nature reserve on Dartmoor. We haven't yet visited it, but we know that the path runs by a river and that there should be plenty of spring daffodils out. I am curious to know what to expect, and even how I should dress for it. So I ask the question "How will our walk turn out today?" Then I pick out three cards: Temperance, the Tower, and the Star. Right—there are two cards with an abundance of water! I'm guessing that the river will be high and that we'll probably have to splash through some flooded parts too. The Tower bothers me a little, and I'll take it as a warning that we should take care not to trip and fall over any unstable boulders. Rocks falling on our heads, such as those that come cascading down from the Tower, are unlikely in this context, but loose stones causing a hazard are a distinct possibility.

Later, we are home from our walk and I consider the reading. There was plenty of flowing water, and it was wet underfoot in places too. The meadows by the river were carpeted with wild daffodils, and I realize that they are the stars in the card, though I need to stretch a point slightly, as the flowers are six-petaled and the stars are eight-pointed. However, the image, with its golden beauty, really does correspond to my experience seeing thousands of daffodils today. As for the Tower, I didn't experience any kind of fall, but nevertheless I am very glad that I saw it as a warning and took a walking pole, since the path was slippery and stony in places.

This is one aspect of card reading where we may never know whether a warning or a piece of advice averted an unhappy outcome. But better safe than sorry, and a good fortune-teller should be happy when perceived potential misfortune doesn't occur, even if it means that the reading wasn't so strikingly accurate after all. As Glyn, my Tarot master, told me, "The reading shows what the outcome of a situation is likely to be if things carry on as they are at the moment. It doesn't mean that there is no choice in the matter." Even the simplest version of fortune-telling usually offers the chance to change the pattern of events if we grasp that opportunity.

THE FOUR-CARD READING

If you'd like to extend this three-card method a little, or you want to add more structure, you can do a four-card reading. This is better done sitting at a table, or by some surface that you can place the cards on carefully to preserve their positions.

As before, start by establishing the question. Once the cards have been shuffled, ask the querent to select just one card from the pack. This will act as the significator of the reading. Then ask him or her to pick the other three cards, and lay them out from left to right, in the order that they were drawn, at a little distance from the significator. It would also be valid to lay out the top three cards from the deck, rather than asking the querent to pick them from the fan. Decide beforehand which method you wish to use, and if you choose to turn over three cards in order from the top of the deck, make sure that the cards get a thorough shuffling first. Having the querent pick three cards separately may be more suitable in a context where there isn't the time or perhaps the space to do the shuffling effectively. You will see from this choice that there can be flexibility in the rules, provided that variations are in keeping with the situation and the intention of the reading.

Evaluating the Cards

When evaluating the cards, keep to the same kind of approach as the three-card reading—that is, make the reading relatively simple and not too serious.

The significator generally represents the person or the nature of the question asked. However, for a "cameo" reading, it is more practical to combine this and to say that this card will represent the person and their current state or preoccupation.

The three cards can be read as past, present, and future, from left to right. Let's take an imaginary reading for a woman in her thirties. She draws:

Significator: the Lover

Cards: the Sun, the Devil, the High Priestess

Her question, she says, is about a current relationship. As reader, you can deduce that she is undecided what to do, as signified by the Lover, who is making a choice. In the past, you can see that everything was open and happy (the Sun), but now she feels constrained by her situation (the Devil). Your advice might be that she needs to take back possession of her independence and rely more on her own inner wisdom (the High Priestess). The cards indicate that she might end up on her own, but it's quite possible that once she's righted the balance, and regained her confidence, she can handle the difficulties in the relationship.

I'd like to emphasize that this is a hypothetical reading, and depending on the person involved and the exact voicing of the question, you might see different aspects of these cards coming into play. Note, too, that the outcome is not fixed; the relationship could go either way, so it's not a simple yes/no result. As I've just suggested, divination is not necessarily the perception of a fixed future. The diviner should give the person somewhere further to go; the aim is that by seeing the situation more clearly, choices also become more apparent, and the querent is better placed to make those decisions and work with their strengths, in harmony with his or her inner nature. Even with a simple reading such as this one, this level of significance comes into play.

REVERSALS

Some Tarot practitioners use reversals to denote an opposite of the core meaning of the cards; in other words, the cards are shuffled in such a way that they could turn up in either orientation—right-side up or upside-down—and a reversal would be seen as a weakening of the positive or negative elements of the cards. My divination practice does not include reversals of the cards. In all the readings that I cover in this book, the cards are always placed right-side up. As a Tarot reader, my relationship with the cards is with the core symbol, and I don't wish to dilute that by introducing shifts that veil the prime meaning of the card. Reversals seem to me like a kind of intellectual overlay, which can come between you and the intimate experience of the card. However, the choice will be yours, and you should find that recommendations for layouts and interpretations in this book can be used with reversals if you so wish.

So at this point, we've completed the foundation of Tarot reading. The wandering fortune-teller is now equipped to take her cards to a party, lay them out on a market stall, and do a swift reading where and when circumstances require. This is the basis of Tarot reading, and although we shall look at the cards in more depth now, and study the approach of the Fool's Mirror readings, it always pays to know the craft at its practical level.

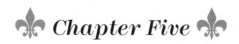

Chapter Five

BECOMING THE DIVINER— GRASPING THE FOOL'S MIRROR

"In patterns innocently captured, you can read the imprint of cosmic purpose and events that are coming to pass. I call this the Fool's Mirror." This was how Glyn, my Tarot teacher, spoke to me about divination near the end of his life. He first taught me his approach to Tarot over thirty years before that, but only now did he name this as the Fool's Mirror. I see this now as the culmination of a legacy, an emblem that helped me to make sense of what I had learned and provided me with a way to pass on this knowledge to other Tarot readers and diviners. I cannot say how long he had this in mind, whether it was a late-flowering symbol for the kind of approach that he used or it was implicit in what he had been taught by a Tarot master before him. Whatever its origins, it is a name, a symbol, and an approach that I should now like to share with you.

THE FOOL'S MIRROR SCHOOL OF DIVINATION

In this chapter, we will investigate the practice of Fool's Mirror Tarot in depth, starting with a distillation of the approach, summarized as a set of guidelines, and followed with a one-by-one exploration of each Tarot card, its historical associations, and possible interpretations. In chapter six, we will look at the significance of numbering and structure in the Tarot pack, and in chapter seven we move on to the important Fool's Mirror layout that uses all twenty-two Tarot Triumphs, with instructions for reading this spread. In chapter eight, we continue the study of how to manage a Tarot reading and consider important issues of ethics, energies, and responsibility. Finally, in chapter nine, the way opens up to a creative exploration of Tarot, using exercises and personal talents to give individual expression to its symbolism.

The Fool and His Mirror

In the Fool's Mirror approach, the Tarot cards themselves act as the mirror, the means of reflecting the pattern of events. The question posed for the reading stands as the frame of the mirror, setting the scope for what is revealed. The handle symbolizes the intention of the diviner, who holds the mirror steady so that the pattern shows up with clarity. But it is the eye, the mind, and the heart of the diviner, that acts to interpret that pattern with an observant, contemplative, and sympathetic engagement. The mirror is the tool, not the meaning of Tarot itself.

This emblem of the fool with his mirror is not so much an extension of the Tarot card of the Fool, but a version of the archetypal fool, who uses his mirror to reflect both truth and folly. In the Tarot card, the Fool does not in fact usually carry a mirror, but he does in some cultural representations of his role as jester. In one traditional German carnival, for instance, a whole procession of fools dances through the town, all of them holding up mirrors for the onlookers to see and reflect upon their own divine folly.[1]

In a Fool's Mirror Tarot reading, each of us takes on the guise of this fool in an innocent quest for meaning. With the cards as a mirror, we can hold up a reflecting surface to the universe and witness the forms and designs captured there. We aspire to do this for others too; the job of fool-as-Tarot-reader is to enable someone to perceive the situation that the mirror captures and to gain a little perspective on it. Perhaps, with good intention and a little luck, we will be able to convey this with wisdom too. Our knowledge of the Tarot helps us to interpret the cards, and by going further, and simply beholding that reflection, we may also touch on a deeper level of knowledge coming from a greater source of consciousness.

The Fool's Mirror thus symbolizes the act of divination, and in terms of Tarot, this approach requires a deeper understanding of the Tarot cards than the simple interpretations considered earlier. Instinctive responses to the Triumphs on parade, followed by key interpretations of each card, lay the foundation; but reflecting on the cards in a more rounded way, as we are about to do, will give the depth of understanding needed to wield the Fool's Mirror effectively. This can mean trying to encompass the sometime contradictory meanings of an image as well as its diverse historical associations. In a "reflective" type of view, paradoxes often supplant straightforward definitions. But if we are willing to take this approach, then we can absorb the archetypal nature of each card, admitting it to the inner sanctum of our own psyche. And this way, too, any reading we give can be truly responsive to the needs of the situation, generated from the depths of our own understanding rather than from stock interpretations.

Before we investigate each Tarot Trump in depth, though, I will set out a guide to the Fool's Mirror approach, in which the essential points of this school of Tarot are set out. All these ideas are brought out in the main text of this book, but here they are rounded up and presented as the twelve faces of the Fool's Mirror.

THE TWELVE FACES OF THE FOOL'S MIRROR

1. The Fool holds up his mirror to reflect the pattern of the cosmos for this moment in time. Then, as the Fool or diviner, in patterns innocently captured, you can read the imprint of cosmic purpose and events that are coming to pass. The Fool stands for the innocent openness of the diviner, using in this case the Tarot cards as a mirror to reflect the pattern of events.

2. The Fool's Mirror diviner is willing to use all the cards in the Major Arcana when the context is appropriate. The twenty-two Trumps are an entity, just as all the signs of the zodiac are contained in an astrological horoscope. They each have their part to play in forming the picture of the moment. It is the way they are arranged that defines what that picture may be.

3. No card in the twenty-two Trumps is intrinsically "good" or "evil." All have their positive and negative qualities. It depends upon their position in the layout and the intuitive understanding of the diviner to see how this is weighted in any one reading.

4. In this approach, embrace paradox rather than avoid it. If there are apparently contradictory meanings, both in individual cards and in the Tarot layout, the aim is to extend awareness so as to encompass both ends of the paradox and perceive what its overall significance might be.

5. The Fool can be wise or foolish, playful or serious. The Fool embodies these qualities, which is how the diviner should approach the practice of Tarot reading. The act of raising the mirror—laying out the cards—is a serious one, but the mind must be nimble and creative in interpreting the results.

6. In contemplating the cards, aspire to contact that "common mind," a greater source of consciousness that may help to determine the significance of the Tarot Trumps in a reading. This means that set interpretations are often not appropriate, since much depends on how the twenty-two Trumps are configured in a particular reading, and how you perceive the wholeness of the reading.

7. As the Tarot reader, endeavor to put personal feelings and preconceptions out of the way so that the pattern in the mirror can reflect as clearly as possible, without distortion.

8. The Fool's Mirror is not a purely psychic approach to divination, and it needs a good basis of study and

practice to work from, plus a solid knowledge of Tarot symbolism.

9. Take responsibility for what you say; you do not own the reading, but you are liable for the way it is imparted. At the same time, though, you are only part of the equation and are not the sole reason why a reading may or may not be productive.

10. The moment of divination, of holding up the Fool's mirror, is important. Acknowledge the importance of that moment by paying conscious attention to what is happening.

11. Give the ritual of the reading its due, however you decide to set that up. There is no specific overriding external ritual attached to Fool's Mirror Tarot divination. In fact, it is important to have a flexible approach, to adapt to different conditions, times, and places. However, ritual is a positive tool, and it helps to focus intent and to create good conditions in that moment.

12. Enjoy your experience with the Tarot! Remember that it is creative play, and you are something of a fool, not a magus. Be creative, unconventional if you wish, and willing to experience joy, awe, or whatever other emotions come your way. The reflection in the Fool's Mirror is eternally changing, although our grasp on the mirror must be steady, and our intention held firm.

TAROT AS ARCHETYPE

As we now enter this Fool's Mirror level of Tarot reading, I suggest that you review the definitions and descriptions of the first two stages (the procession of Triumphs in chapter one and the keynotes in chapter three), and make sure that you are familiar with them. Then, take time to consider each card in more depth through the portraits that follow. You can use your own Tarot pack to contemplate each card in turn, in association with the descriptions given here, or refer to the illustrations in this book (see pp. 102). Even if you are already very familiar with Tarot, it does not hurt to revisit it in reflective mode; this can generate new insights or remind you of ones that have slipped out of mind. During the writing of this book, I took the opportunity to give myself a day to reflect on each card. This, combined with rereading my old notes on the cards, really refreshed my vision and brought back earlier insights that I had completely forgotten.

INTERPRETATIONS

These interpretations are based on my understanding of the cards as it as evolved over the years, supplemented by historical research and other studies of Tarot. I have had to restrict my enthusiasm for writing about each card, though, and keep it in proportion to the book as a whole, which means that certain historical allusions have been relegated to endnotes. (I do recommend a trawl through these.) I have also focused on what I consider to be core meanings, rather than following too many enticing trails of speculation. Not all of the descriptions that follow are the same length because some need more explanation and historical background, while a more compact exposition serves others better.

I also write about each card as though it applies to the present or the future of the question asked. Tarot symbols are of course often signs of what is to come, or at least an indication of how things are likely to develop from the current situation. However, in a full reading that encompasses past, present, and future, cards may point out what has already happened, or what the situation is that underlies the present time, based on earlier events and attitudes. So, for instance, while the Tower can indicate a sudden change that will happen, it may also, according to its position, symbolize a radical change of circumstances that has already taken place. The interpretations given in this chapter are templates and must be further assessed in the context of the reading.

Likewise, in a full Fool's Mirror reading, or any other kind of full Tarot spread, each card is modified by its relationship to the other cards. From the juxtaposition of the cards, and their specific combinations, the Tarot reader shapes the interpretation and delivers the narrative of the reading.

CARDS USED

The imagery I refer to in the descriptions that follow is that of the traditional Marseilles Tarot Triumphs. The main pack that I use here is the Grimaud deck (republished c. 1969), but I have referred widely to reproductions of other historic packs in my possession, especially the Conver deck of 1761, the Pierre Madénie from Dijon 1709, an eighteenth-century Italian Bologna pack, and the Golden Tarot version of the Visconti-Sforza fifteenth-century deck. I have also studied a multitude of digital images of historical Tarot packs, mostly sourced from the British Museum, including the so-called Charles VI pack in the Bibliothèque Nationale de France and the important 1650 Vieville set.[2]

NAMES FOR THE TRIUMPHS

I mainly use the English names for the cards that accord with the Grimaud Marseilles pack. One exception is my substitution of Strength for Force. It looks as though the manufacturers simply repeated the French word in their English-language version, but *force* in French means *strength* in English, and this difference is very important in the interpretation of the card.

I have kept the title Pope, however, rather than substitute the rather grandiose term Hierophant, which is sometimes used, or even High Priest. I feel that these take us too far away from the original meaning of a public figure of religious authority. The Pope is a figure we are all familiar with, even though he has limited impact in today's world, compared to Renaissance Europe. As I have mentioned, the papal figures were too much for some Protestant regions, which replaced both cards with the classical deities Juno and Jupiter. I have retained the High Priestess, as the Grimaud pack does, rather than use versions such as the female pope or Papess, both odd and somewhat clumsy in English. Although female pope might match Pope as nomenclature, I believe that High Priestess represents her function better and is more in line with what was intended at the time, as we shall see shortly.

The Fool

In the Tarot image, the Fool is both jester and beggar. His cap and bells are those of the court fool, but his ragged breeches, traveling staff, and tiny bundle of worldly goods are more in keeping with those of a hand-to-mouth wanderer. The little dog is probably his companion, although some Tarot interpreters see it as a dog chasing him out of the neighborhood that he passes through on his rambles. But they are more likely to be a pair; the Fool and his dog are often found together in medieval pictures. Historically, the Fool or jester was a very important character. His job was to deflate pomposity, to speak the truth when no one else dared, and to lighten up tension with cheeky humor. At the time of the earliest known Tarot cards, in fifteenth-century Italy, the employment of a fool or jester was at its peak of popularity, so this image would have been well known to early users of the Tarot.[3]

The Fool has always remained without a number in the Marseilles Tarot pack, as far as I am aware, and has only been shown as zero in modern versions of Tarot, such as the Rider-Waite pack.[4] He therefore stands outside the twenty-one numbered cards and can be seen as both beginning and end of the pack, or even as standing at the center while the others process around him in a circle. In a way, the Fool is the key to the whole Tarot pack and can butt in anywhere he pleases. He represents the human quest and the eternal optimism of the seeker. He can be foolish, but, like a child, he offers a fresh view of the truth, undermining that which is false. The Fool is the blind spot of our nature—we can see ahead and behind but can never quite make out where we are. He is the human error factor that is never entirely ruled out, despite our best efforts with technology. In relation to the other twenty-one cards, he is not one of them, but contains their potentialities within him.

The Fool is always traveling. He can be perfectly innocent or perfectly ignorant, depending upon how you look at him, but he is there within all of us. As a wild card, he is best placed to represent the significator in a reading, and if he turns up in this position, it's a sign that the querent is genuinely open to hearing what the Tarot has to say.

And, of course, the Fool is allied to the Fool's Mirror in the context of this school of Tarot. Who is more innocent than the Fool, in holding up a mirror to the universe? But also who is more ready to laugh with innocent merriment at the follies that appear there?

1. The Magician

The colorful figure of the Magician is the first of the Tarot Triumphs to take the stage in the numbered sequence of cards. He can perform wonderful tricks, and he knows the secrets of making things appear and disappear, and even how to turn one thing into something entirely different. The Magician can transform the humdrum into the exotic. He brightens up people's lives when they gather to watch him perform, and he sets their minds working, wondering "How on earth did he do that?"

In French, his name is Le Bateleur, or Juggler, but although this name appears on most of the traditional Marseilles packs, his role in the Tarot is primarily that of a conjuror or magician. Taking both terms in a slightly wider sense, he is a prime candidate for one of the possible jongleurs in this pack, a strolling player who could turn his hand to all different kinds of entertainment: conjuring tricks, taming beasts, acting, storytelling, and performing music.[5] This kind of adaptability is also one of the marks of a true magician who can create wonderful effects by using whatever simple things are at hand, improvising to delight a crowd. Ritual and magic go hand in hand: the laying out of his equipment on the table, the gathering of everyone's attention, and the clever use of words and gestures will all help to create enchantment. Sometimes this is based on illusion, sometimes it appears to be real magic. It depends on what we believe is possible.

As a Tarot Triumph, the image represents the tapping of energy and ways of directing this force with precision and skill. To keep this flow of creation going, however, one has to recognize that all the things one can achieve in this world are, ultimately, games and illusions. But play, color, and delight accompany this revelation. On the Magician's table, in many versions of the card, we see the tools that are considered to represent the four elements, continuously in movement, forming different combinations every moment. The dice or counters stand for earth, the cups for water, the knife for fire, and the wand for air. The Magician knows how to make the best of all the opportunities that each of these moments affords.

The card can signify inspiration, which seems to come out of thin air, like the balls that the Magician produces. It can also indicate a flair for business and making money. In some cases it may mean deceit, trickery, or even being caught on the sharp edge of one's own cleverness. So the person in question could be a confidence trickster, or someone who knows how to "cast the glamour," the old gypsy trick of hypnotizing a crowd so that they believed they saw something quite different from reality—for example, a cockerel carrying the trunk of an oak tree in his beak instead of a wisp of straw.[6]

As number 1, the Magician leads the whole procession of Tarot Trumps that follow. Perhaps there is a clue embodied in the dice sometimes shown on his table. For throws of two dice, there are twenty-one possible combinations; the casting of the Magician's dice may therefore create all the twenty-one numbered cards of the Triumphs.[7] The Magician thus opens the way to the sequence of Triumphs.

2. The High Priestess

The image of the High Priestess, otherwise called the Papess, or female Pope, is very simple in one sense. A woman with a tall headdress sits before a curtain hung between two pillars, holding an open book in her lap. But she has aroused great debate and much research among Tarot historians.[8] Does she represent Pope Joan, Isis, Sophia, the Virgin Mary, Faith and the Church, a prophetic Sibyl, a sorceress, or pagan knowledge? All have been proposed as candidates, along with a specific historical character: the heretical Manfreda, who believed in creating female popes. She was a thirteenth-century cousin of the Visconti family, who later commissioned one of the first Tarot packs. After fighting my way through this thicket of possible allusions and appraising their possibilities, I have arrived at the view that this card can best be understood not as one particular figure, but as an embodiment of wisdom and ancient knowledge symbolized in female form.

In the early Renaissance, for practitioners of philosophical or Hermetic traditions, such a figure of female wisdom was not only acceptable but also essential to their cosmology. The headdress and book of the High Priestess were associated with the spirit of ancient teaching, and from that standpoint she could quite readily have been equated by different interpreters with Mary, Sophia, Isis, or the kabbalistic Shekinah,[9] each a feminine representation of wisdom, and each current in different strands of teaching and thinking at the time.[10] It is very unlikely, however, that the High Priestess would represent Pope Joan, an object of mockery, or Manfreda, a condemned heretic.[11] She is not a historical counterpart of the Pope, either, or a renegade version of the Pope in female form. There is a case for associating her with Prudence, a later personification of Sophia, the spirit of

Wisdom; some of her attributes—book and triple crown, for instance—can be found in imagery related to Prudence.[12, 13]

So the High Priestess is a teacher of wisdom. She can thus be perceived in different ways, according to inclination; she could indeed be an ancient goddess (Isis), or a female personification of the presence of God (Shekinah), or of wisdom (Sophia), or of spiritual birth (Mary). You may prefer to see her in the guise of one association rather than another, and very likely that was true too for others using the Tarot in past centuries. But if you go past the trappings, you can also see her as the symbol of contemplation itself. She sits at the entrance to the temple and is the keeper of its mysteries. In a reading, the card may suggest the need to tap one's inner resources and to use silence wisely. Intuition, patience, and a considered approach are recommended, and restraint rather than thoughtless action.

3. The Empress

The Empress is the highest female authority in worldly terms; she helps to guard the order of civilization and represents the power of the land. But also, her role as the mother of heirs is implicit; there is often a strong hint of pregnancy in the card's image. She is therefore in a sense both a kind of earth mother, with the warmth and nurturing that this implies, and the strict keeper of human rules. The juxtaposition of these qualities is in fact not unlike those found in ordinary motherhood, where a mother has a close instinctive bond with her child, but also establishes, in a considered way, patterns of routine to govern behavior and help the child's development. The Empress, therefore, can both be seen as a stern, controlling woman and also one of fertility and sexuality. Attempting to understand both sides of her nature leads us deeper into the significance of the symbol.[14]

The Empress is a female figurehead of the physical world, in contrast with the High Priestess as the female authority of the inner life. The Empress's popularity among her people does not depend entirely on an external show of pomp and pageantry, but also on the way she is seen handling her private domain in palace or castle. The equivalent in modern times is the hunger of the public for details of the private lives of the royals. Ruling an empire successfully requires creating a certain rapport with one's subjects, and the skillful Empress will understand just how much of her personality to display and what to keep private. A monarch who tries to conceal her domestic life completely will be perceived as rigid, arrogant, and unreal. However, she has to conceal certain things; she has to hide her personal feelings for much of the time, and she must not show weakness unless it is advantageous for her to do so. Her personal and public strength, therefore, is built through these tests and rigors.

For her imperial role, she has all the trappings: a throne, a shield, and a scepter. She forms the counterpart of the Emperor, each fulfilling a different but complementary function in the game of human conquest and the establishment of social order. Therefore, the Empress in Tarot interpretation is first and foremost a woman of power, with the right to punish or reward. She can represent the boss, the team leader, or a dominant female relative, for instance. But her femininity is never totally eclipsed by her official role, and she is also a symbol of the need to mate and marry, and to raise children in a structured situation. She is a reminder that love has consequences, and that power must be exercised responsibly. In a reading, the card may point to some kind of concealment in a situation, or a strong front that hides something fragile or vulnerable.

4. The Emperor

The Emperor and the Empress are clearly a pair, and they represent the highest order of monarchs, exceeding the rank of king and queen. Their historical associations, as perceived by early Tarot makers and users, hark back to the might of the Roman Empire and the subsequent reign of the Holy Roman Empire, which started with the crowning of Charlemagne by the Pope in 800 CE. The office was still in place, just about, at the time the Tarot emerged, and the images of Emperor and Empress are thus clear symbols of supreme temporal reign, governing the things of this earth that lie within their empire, and upheld in their position by the spiritual approval of the Pope.

As the Empress expresses the feminine rule, so the Emperor represents masculine power and authority. His image in profile is more formal, indicating a greater aloofness, and he looks forward, indicating that he is maintaining a sense of direction. His progress is more focused and controlled, as he is not hampered in his movements by the demands of childbirth. As a father figure, the Emperor carries the qualities of detached love, a love that can be stern as well as compassionate. His will is keen and concentrated. He is not likely to be swayed by personal considerations, but he may fall into temptations of abuse of power, use of cruelty, or a desire for revenge. The card may be a warning as to the strength of one's own power, and a reminder to use it justly and sparingly. In a reading, it may represent destiny, or a path to follow.

Taken as a pair, the Emperor and the Empress may have an association with the allegorical king and queen of alchemy, who represent, among other things, gold and silver. Their union symbolizes the "completion of the Great Work."[15] Whether or not this is an intentional part of Tarot symbolism, their pairing can be seen as the mystical marriage of male and female, and if they turn up close together in a reading, it is a very strong sign of success or achievement.

Their eagle-emblazoned shields may be simply a tradition of the Byzantine rulers, but they could also bear classical allusions, which would be in keeping with early Renaissance imagery. The eagle was the bird of Zeus, and as the eagles usually face in different directions on the shields, they may represent the god's two golden eagles, which Zeus let loose to fly around the world and to meet again at its center.[16] Between them, we could therefore say that the Emperor and Empress create a kind of universal center, where their own two eagles face each other.[17] So although the Emperor and the Empress appear to be conventional representations of earthly rulers, in fact their trappings and their roles indicate their power is as archetypes, as well as heads of state.

5. The Pope

The Pope and the High Priestess are both cards about knowledge, but the difference is this: the High Priestess sits directly before the veil, which marks the entrance to the inner sanctum, while the Pope is enthroned some distance from the two pillars of the holy temple. (The traditional images are reasonably consistent in this respect.) So, whereas the High Priestess is a symbol of direct contact with the inner mysteries, the Pope represents spiritual authority outside of the sanctuary. He is empowered to give blessings.[18] He is also a teacher, as witnessed by the little figures who kneel in front of him; it was common at the time to represent the image of a spiritual master or teacher as much larger than that of his followers.[19] The Pope is thus a giant to his disciples, just as an important teacher can loom large in our lives, remaining as a permanent inner signpost to guide us long after contact has ceased. A teacher may take on a role as a kind of superman or superwoman who can at times be a wonderful support along the way, but at others an obstacle to making our own discoveries. I think many of us recollect teaching figures of authority from our past who have inhibited our progress rather than advancing it. The Pope can therefore be a symbol of the transmission of knowledge through a recognized chain of authority, but his teaching can become dogma and his dictates fossilize into rigid mandates.

Needless to say, the Pope in a Tarot reading does not have to represent any specific religious leader or even organized religion; he is more of a teacher or instructor, a guiding figure in any particular situation. He is likely to signify what you or the querent consider to be a higher form of authority, the person who holds the balance of power or the moral high ground. The card can also represent the inner values that you depend on and the dictates that you have absorbed and live your life by. We all have values that are to some extent conditioned, often imprinted at an early age, and that help us to live responsibly; sometimes, though, these may conflict with the stirrings of true conscience, and so the card could represent an ethical clash within oneself or with an outside figure of moral authority.

Overall, this is a card of teaching, listening, and learning. It also represents the way we formulate truth, and the ideas that we hold dear. In its less favorable aspects, the image can signify being too dependent upon advice or ritual and convention. In a more general sense, it can represent the culture we have been brought up in, the lessons we have learned, and the rules we live by. The Pope has the power to assist us in becoming strong and wise, but he may also represent the domination of external ideas and principles over our own individuality.

6. The Lover

The Marseilles version of the Lover clearly indicates a choice: which woman will the young man decide to marry? Some earlier versions, notably the fifteenth-century Visconti-Sforza pack, show what appears to be a wedding in progress; and in that particular case, the figures are presumed to be Francesco Sforza and Bianca Maria Visconti. The couple married in 1441, and the sumptuous set of Tarot cards may have actually been commissioned for their wedding.[20] But the dilemma shown on the prevailing image in the Marseilles Triumph is not a straightforward, happy union; as with many of the cards, it poses a question for us to fathom.

One common interpretation is that these two ladies represent Vice (sometimes called Sensuality) and Virtue. This is borne out by various emblems independent of Tarot packs, such as the one in *Orbis Sensualium Pictus* by Comenius (1658), where his illustration no. 109 under "Moral Philosophy" shows much the same picture, with the two women positively tugging the young man in different directions![21] Comenius's written description here encompasses the teaching of Pythagoras on the importance of wise choices: "This Life is a way, or a place divided into two ways, like Pythagoras's Letter Y. Broad, on the left hand track; narrow, on the right; that belongs to Vice, this to Virtue." So there is, perhaps, a kind of implicit sacred geometry embedded here with the forking symbol of lover and ladies indicating the diverging pathways.

The Marseilles Tarot version of the Lover is a masterpiece of cross tensions, though, within this Y-shaped formation. Here, Cupid's arrow points toward the man's left, and to the fair-haired maiden standing there. The Lover, though, looks to the right, toward the laurel-crowned lady with the severe face. She rests a restraining hand on his right shoulder, her left reaching out to him below, while the pretty girl on the left, in some versions crowned with flowers,[22] touches his heart with her fingers. She looks forward, while Miss Laurel Crown looks straight into the Lover's eyes. Both seem to say, "He's mine!"

This more complex version of the Lover, rather than simply representing a wedding scene, is the kind of image that lends such depth and subtlety of interpretation to the Tarot. Is love ever straightforward, after all? People who ask for a reading are often nursing a burning issue about love, which may be full of complexities. The diviner's role may be to try to see the simpler choices lying within that issue, rather in the same way that the Y shape helps to make sense of all the cross currents in the Tarot image. Often it comes down to asking, "What do you really want?" The card may not always be about a relationship, but it can also indicate a decision pending, a choice to be made in another area of life. Likewise, it could indicate a matter of choosing a particular path and sacrificing another way forward, however tempting, in order to achieve the desired goal.

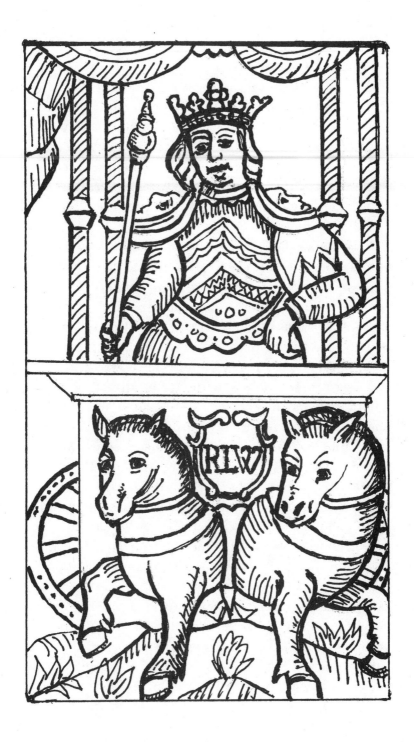

7. The Chariot

The Chariot is one of those cards that is not too difficult to grasp simply by looking at the image. Here we have drive, energy, and movement. The crowned and armed youth rides in a triumphal car, a classical Roman emblem of victory. This card in a reading can signify achievement and the overcoming of obstacles, which sometimes requires battle. "Onward! Forward!" is the war cry here. The chariot can never go backward—something to ponder in its overall meaning.

There is also allegory here: the harnessing of the horses represents control over our own emotional power. Once we have that control, we can move forward with confidence. Feelings such as anger, desire, and excitement make terrible masters but excellent servants. Curiously though, the driver does not seem to have reins. Once again a Tarot card poses a question: how can he steer and restrain his horses without the direct control of reins? Perhaps the message is that once emotions are understood, and put to work productively, then the trio of instinct, feeling, and rational consciousness (chariot, horses, master-driver) can travel forward together in harmony, without overt control. But although the charioteer, who may be a prince, might be proud, even arrogant, he is not complacent. He wears armor, recognizing that protection is often necessary, since blind trust may come to grief, and treachery is to be found in unexpected places. He must remain watchful, self-reliant, alert, and prepared. But we in turn also need to keep watch over him, for the charioteer, if wrongly motivated, can be cruel and proud and ride roughshod over others.

Plato made use of the charioteer as an allegory of the human struggle, portraying it as one where we try to control a pair of horses who want to go in different directions; one is of a finer breed and represents our noble urges and impulse toward truth, while the other is a brute beast, fixated on selfish appetites. This classical reference might well have been understood by Renaissance owners of Tarot packs after Plato's writings began to be reintroduced into Europe in the late fifteenth century, and it could be a conscious element in the evolution of Tarot's design, though it was probably not the only source for the image.

Historically, too, the image has similarities to the triumphal chariots that were still used in processions or as allegorical emblems in early Renaissance times. One early Marseilles-style pack, known as the Vieville Tarot dating from 1650, shows sphinxes drawing the chariot. This is the only traditional pack that I have seen with sphinxes, but the idea was certainly carried forward into the nineteenth-century Oswald Wirth pack and then into the influential Rider-Waite pack a couple of decades later. Digging a little deeper, I find that Renaissance representation of myth did include triumphal chariots drawn by strange creatures, especially sphinxes or lions.[23]

Sphinxes were portrayed as part human, part lion and were said to symbolize the duality of wisdom and ignorance. This fits in well with the idea of self-mastery and the need to control opposing forces that the symbol of the Chariot implies. Lions, on the other hand, were sometimes used to pull the car of Cupid, whom we have just met in the preceding card, the Lover. Lions pulling a chariot were also designated as vice or virtue in some representations. Could this card, the Chariot, therefore be a development of the previous one, the Lover, with his attempt to choose between pleasure and true union?[24]

Taken at face value, our princely charioteer may simply be who he seems to be: a noble or royal warrior commanding his chariot. Go deeper, and we can see him as an emblem of the human condition and the task of channeling our passions and abilities. Consider his place in the pack, and perhaps this opens up a further perspective, one where the raw emotions of the Lover have now evolved into the task of self-mastery. At any rate, his proud presence comes through strongly, and he symbolizes the control and drive that need to be kept on track but can achieve winning results.

8. Justice

The figure of Justice, as depicted in Tarot, is familiar to most of us. We know the way she sits with her sword pointing upward in her right hand and the scales balanced from her left. She is a representation of Iustitia, or Lady Justice, the Roman goddess, although the concept of divine or personified justice coupled with a pair of scales goes back further. In ancient Egypt, every person was said to undergo an elaborate judgment ritual after death to have their past deeds scrutinized by the gods. This involved entering the Hall of Truth and having their hearts weighed in the scales of justice. In the most common image we have of Justice today, she is blindfolded, but in the Tarot card she is shown with her eyes open. This in fact affirms the late medieval origins of Tarot, as the idea of depicting Justice blindfolded did not begin to appear until the fifteenth century.

Justice is one of the four cardinal virtues, a schema originating in Platonic thought and taken up by the Christian Church. Of the other three, Temperance already has a place in the Tarot pack; Strength may double for Fortitude, and, as already suggested, the High Priestess could serve as the fourth virtue, Prudence. Some Tarot experts consider it very important to find the full complement of the virtues in the Tarot pack, to prove that they were part of its schema right from the start.[25] But no one has yet managed to prove that the Tarot is founded on a straightforward series of religious or philosophical allusions.[26] Tarot is an extraordinary mix of images and concepts, and this gives it its power. It is symbolic rather than allegorical, and it cannot be pinned down to a single set of meanings. So although Justice is one of the more straightforward and recognizable images in the pack, it is worthy of exploration afresh to penetrate its deeper meanings and implications that might not immediately be obvious.

We can see justice operating in every human society, and although the principle is universal, each culture devises its own system of justice. Whether a person is a member of a tribe or a citizen of a great country, he or she is required to know what its laws are. Infringement of those laws brings some kind of punishment, or compulsory restitution, and this highlights the overt function of Justice as Tarot Triumph, that of setting the balance of the scales to rights. The ways of implementing this range from the imposing law courts of capital cities to a group of tribal elders gathered to decide how many cattle the miscreant should pay to compensate the man he has wronged. In families too, parents act as enforcers of Justice, handing out rewards and withdrawing privileges, often battling with the growing child's own very particular sense of what is fair, and what is not. So although Justice may proceed irrevocably once its due process is started, it may not always placate or satisfy the victim or restore and redeem the lives of those on whose behalf it acts. Justice is not perfect; many who begin legal proceedings for justice may come to wish they had never started. So it is not always a straightforward, clear-cut force for good, and the Tarot Triumph may warn us not to invoke the goddess of Justice unless we are willing to let her do her work, whatever the result may be.

In a reading, Justice could refer directly to legal matters, arbitration, or the means of correcting a balance in any context—particularly rights and wrongs. But it also represents the laws operating in our personal lives. As we sow, we shall reap. Recognizing what kind of seeds there are, and how to sow and cultivate them, is something that we can actively pursue. It is often said that everyone is dealt a hand of cards in life, but it's how you play them that matters. Knowledge of our own strengths and weaknesses can help us to use them productively and work within the range of possible achievements, instead of hankering after the impossible. Justice points to the pattern of cause and effect and invites us to learn its laws.

9. The Hermit

On the face of it, the Hermit seems to be one of the simpler images of the Tarot. He is the solitary seeker searching for truth away from the merry-go-round of the world's affairs, carrying his own light in the form of a lantern. He wears a coarse but practical cloak, which gives him adequate protection from the cold. The cloak is also a symbol of simplicity and poverty; it guards him against robbers, who see that he has nothing worth stealing, and against any malicious accusations of living too well from the charity of others. In his inner, essential form, he represents the truth-seeker, the person who relies on his own judgment, upheld by deep beliefs and not swayed by riches or glamour. He is, in one sense, the male counterpart to the High Priestess. She renounces family life and takes on a spiritual role as an oracle of wisdom; as stated earlier, she is not in this way the counterpart of the Pope, who represents ecclesiastical authority and the upholding of church law. The Hermit is her equivalent, the man who has become singular, who presents himself naked to the inner truth, shielding himself from the outer world and renouncing its politics. He too may offer wise counsel to others.

Delving a little further into the traditional role of the hermit reveals other facets of his life, which may also help to illuminate his meaning in the Tarot deck. Hermits have been a significant fixture in Christian life since the early centuries. They have not always been solitary, but were sometimes members of orders of "eremites,"[27] and they have served society in different ways, giving something back in return for the privilege of solitude.[28] Hermits often set up their wattle hut, or found a convenient cave, near a crossroads or ford, where they were sought out by travelers for blessings, a night's shelter, and perhaps some wise advice.[29] Perhaps the card of the Hermit conveys a message: you can become solitary, but you will never be completely independent; you can exist only with the goodwill of society, and you will offer something in return for this gift of solitariness and freedom.

There are other possible cultural attributes for the Tarot Hermit too; the lantern he carries may relate to Diogenes, the Greek philosopher and a hermit himself, who famously held up a lamp in broad daylight in his search for an honest man.[30] Or he may be an embodiment of Saturn in his role as Lord of Time, where he appears in some of the earliest Tarot representations with an hourglass instead of a lamp.[31]

Overall, the Hermit represents a quest, a period of retreat, or a time for being alone. Perhaps renunciation is involved, so the card could indicate giving up unnecessary encumbrances. It can also show the emerging of the true self and the willingness to give up pretense. It may, in a spiritual sense, indicate a growing awareness of the soul, but also the recognition of its vulnerability, as a tiny flicker of light. The Hermit knows his life is a small flame, like the one in his lamp, and that an unmeasured vastness lies beyond it. Then, as humbleness grows, so does access to knowledge from a realm much greater than that of individual achievement.

However the Trump needs to be interpreted in a particular situation, it is worth keeping in mind that the Hermit always serves in ways of his own, even if he retreats from the world; solitary prayer, for instance, may have benefits for wider humanity. The lone person is not always a selfish one.

10. The Wheel of Fortune

Since ancient times, human beings have endeavored to understand the cycles that govern our lives—especially those of the sun, moon, and stars. Markings made on bones from at least thirty thousand years ago appear to record cycles of the moon,[32] and later, in the Babylonian era, observatories known as ziggurats were built to study the cycles of the eclipses. From this has come a sense of our own place in the universe, the principles of change at work in our lives, and what can be predicted for us. Writers from Plato to Boethius and Chaucer have all commented upon the way fortune operates in our lives. Allied to this is the sense of cycles of good or bad fortune marking our passage through life; since classical times, the goddess Fortuna with her wheel has been feared and loved in equal measure. The image of Fortune's wheel was widely known by medieval times:

> On Fortune's throne, I used to sit raised up, crowned with the many-colored flowers of prosperity; though I may have flourished, happy and blessed, now I fall from its peak, stripped of glory. The wheel of Fortune turns: I go down, demeaned; now another is raised up. Far too high up sits the king at the summit—let him fear ruin![33]

The corresponding card from one of the earliest known Tarot sets, the Visconti-Sforza, has a piquant series of sayings written in Latin. The first three translate as "I shall reign," "I am reigning," and "I have reigned." These are emblazoned on ribbons attached to figures on the wheel. In this particular depiction of the image, a fourth figure, an old man, is placed under the wheel, declaring piteously, "I have no reign." The Marseilles version just has three figures on the wheel, transmuted into comic figures that mock man's attempt to outwit fortune by imagining themselves great: three monkeys are in rotation, the one who rises up is wearing donkey's ears, and the one at the top sports a crown.

The goddess Fortune remains prominent in our culture today—millions play the lottery each week. And her symbol, the wheel, can also be found in physical form, since the roulette wheel in the casino makes and loses fortunes every day. However, there is more to Fortune's wheel than chance. Cycles are predictable, to some degree. But we still struggle to observe and educate ourselves about those cycles, whether they are to do with menstruation, biorhythms, the economy, or the planetary cycles of astrology interpreted in human terms. We do this in order to forecast these and so avoid disaster, or to turn difficult times to good use. And who turns the handle? Here's another contradiction to ponder. The end of the handle is out of the picture on most of the Marseilles packs. Perhaps it's something that we can grasp and turn for ourselves. Can you create your own luck this way? Maybe. But even if that's not possible all the time—the "lucky" person can become addicted to their own luck and be a victim of its fluctuations—then there may sometimes be a way of stepping back from these effects. Meditation, for instance, is one way of doing this. Or, when we do have to ride the wheel, understanding its inevitable rotation means that we won't expect success, wealth, and beauty to be permanent. Fortune's wheel does not then have the same power to make and break us.

The Wheel of Fortune in a reading does not by itself signify either good or bad luck, but is more about the way that things change. It could indicate any phase in the cycle; it might be time to buy or sell, to take a new step, or just to sit tight and wait until a more propitious moment is right for change. We need to be ready to embrace new opportunities, but also to get off the wheel at the right moment. There is always consolation to be found in the turning of the wheel; at a difficult time in a person's life, you may be able to say to them, "Things will change. Try to find out what you can do to help the process along, but don't worry. The situation will not stay as it is forever."

11. Strength

The usual Tarot representation of Strength is that of a woman bending over a lion and calmly but firmly opening its jaws. The French name for this card is La Force, which indeed means strength, but my Grimaud Marseilles pack keeps the translation as Force in its English version, which seems to be the very opposite of what this card is about. Strength here is definitely not about force in the English sense of the word. Here, gentleness triumphs over brute force, which also sets up one of those intriguing Tarot paradoxes: how can a woman tame such a savage creature without using force? Some earlier versions of Tarot show this card as a woman breaking a pillar in half or a man clubbing a lion, but these are crude allegories by comparison.

To understand this as a tradition, it helps to go right back in human history to the cult of the Mistress of the Beasts. This portrayal of a woman with wild animals, in particular lions, is found in statues and paintings from ancient civilizations such as Crete, Phoenicia, and Mesopotamia. She may be seen standing between lions, riding upon a lion's back, or driving a chariot drawn by lions. So the powerful image of a woman acquiring dominance over these strong and dangerous animals has held sway in human imagination for a very long time. Even the original domestication of animals may have been initiated by the female touch, it has been suggested, when huntsmen brought home orphaned young creatures following a kill and gave them to the women to rear. This does not necessarily give us a historical link to Strength, but it shows that the archetype of woman taming beast resides deep within our culture. It's possible, though, that this image does derive more directly from the woman jongleurs, members of the wandering entertainers who traveled in mixed bands and whose female entertainments included showing and taming wild beasts.[34] Even if the lions were sometimes reported as being "toothless," it was still an awesome spectacle; perhaps the holding open of the mouth was intended to show a skeptical public that the beast did indeed have teeth!

The strength shown, therefore, has an extraordinary power since it overcomes danger through gentleness, patience, and persistence. The woman does not force apart the lion's jaws; the lion sits in submission and allows her to place her hands upon its teeth, the greatest source of potential danger. This indicates a type of strength that works through anything that is not direct force—confidence, compassion, understanding, or quietness. Maybe it could operate too through hypnosis, enchantment, or magic. A sense of timing and the willingness to repeat a process over and over again are other possible implications here; animal training and taming are not for the impatient. Every card offers a lesson to be learnt, and here in psychological terms the task of mastering anger or fear is accomplished by serene persistence.

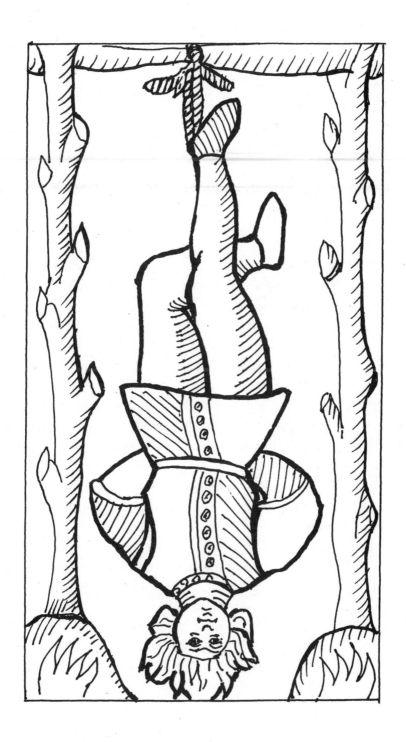

12. The Hanged Man

The Hanged Man may look alarming on first viewing. He is often taken to be a dead man, a criminal who has been hung, or a traitor suspended by his feet according to the Italian custom, and his name at first (Le Pendu in French) seems to support that theory.[35] But the way he is depicted suggests that he is in fact an acrobat. In nearly every version, he looks calm and happy, a man who is in control of what he's doing. Reverse the usual meaning, and you will find a man studying the world in reverse!

There are historical accounts of acrobats and gymnasts who did tricks very much like this, suspended from a rope or a pole. Sometimes they performed high up on the rooftops to entertain visiting dignitaries in Paris or London, astounding them with feats of balance, which included upside-down contortions.[36] An eye-witness account passed on to me in modern times reports seeing an itinerant acrobat in France holding himself in just the same position as the hanged man of the Tarot. There is also a seventeenth-century engraving of acrobats in training, which shows one of them "hanging by one leg with his head downward" from a rope.[37] In a different context, we can find the Tarlà of Girona, a festival still current in northeastern Spain, which involves hanging a life-size dummy dressed as a jester from a pole placed high across the street. He is said to commemorate the dark days of the Black Death in the medieval period, when citizens were confined to their quarters to sit out the plague. To relieve the fear and the tedium, a young acrobat, Tarlà, entertained them with displays of swinging and hanging from these poles.[38] Given that Girona is close to the French border and not too far from Marseilles by sea, it's quite possible that this event was well known along that part of the Mediterranean in Renaissance times.

So in this interpretation of the Hanged Man, we see a figure who chooses to be upside-down and has trained himself to do so. Children love to look at the world the other way up; as a little girl, I used to hang head down off my bed, getting a vivid new perspective of the lino and the fluff balls lying beneath. I've also seen kittens playing similar games. In this light, the main meaning of the card becomes that of skill and balance, and it indicates a willingness to let the usual viewpoint fall away and enter the world of topsy-turvy. The Hanged Man frees himself from conventions. He is also—but not historically, perhaps, in terms of Tarot—the shaman on a vision quest, relinquishing normality to receive gifts of prophecy and healing. This is similar to the description of the ordeal that the Norse god Odin underwent, hanging upside-down from the sacred world tree for nine days and nights, sacrificing himself in order to acquire divine knowledge. Ideas of acrobat and shaman do combine well here, for both are entrusting themselves to a reversal. The acrobat must trust his training and the strength of the rope. The shaman goes willingly into the unknown, ready to be shaped by what he encounters there.

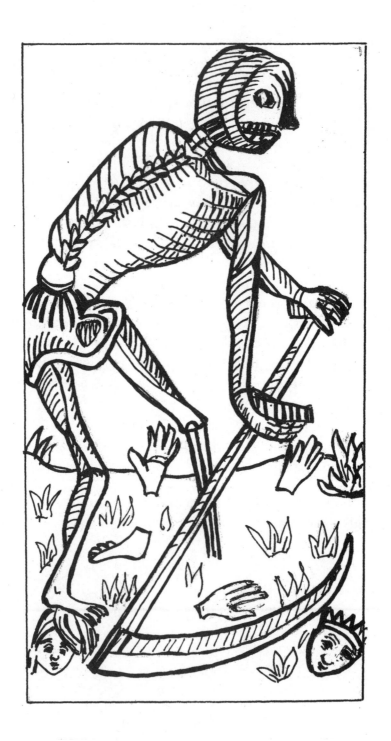

13. Death

In many early Tarot packs, Death was not named. The act of naming might invoke his fearful presence, so it was safer to include him only as an image, along with his number, the so-called "unlucky" thirteen. People were all too aware that the grim reaper with his scythe could strike suddenly, and that he had no pity on those from any station in life. The Dance of Death was a common subject to engrave or paint, with Death cutting a swathe through human society. In the Middle Ages and later, Death was often shown as slaughtering the Pope or Emperor first to make a point that those at the top of society were no more protected from his blow than the poor and humble.[39] However, there was an entertainment value in Death too; then as now, people liked to frighten themselves with the macabre, and the Triumph of Death was a surprisingly popular part of the carnival celebration in the streets. His prevailing image was either that of a skeleton, as here in the Tarot, or his biblical appearance as a "rider on a pale horse."[40] In Northern Italy, the probable birthplace of Tarot, Death rode through the streets on a huge oxcart, accompanied by the Angel of the last Trump.[41]

Death as a Tarot Trump has gained a reputation for bringing dismay and despair to a reading. But nearly all representations of Death in the different Tarot packs show new life springing from the earth around: heads, hands, and plants poke up from the ground. In a considered divination reading, this cycle of death and rebirth or regrowth needs to be taken into account. Death promotes fertility, quite literally, as dead plants and old bones break down and form compost. Nothing is lost, only transformed, so the symbol is not necessarily that of bitter finality. In general, then, we can look to what has been discarded and find valuable resources there. We can also hope for new growth in the future, even when matters seem bleak.

All this, it's plain, can be incorporated into the way we interpret Death in a Tarot reading. It is very rarely an indication of physical human death, and even if such a meaning seems absolutely inevitable to the diviner, I would counsel against proclaiming it as such if it relates to the present or the future in a reading. There is another consideration: if we include all the Tarot Trumps in a layout, as we do in the Fool's Mirror in chapter seven, then we have to see the Death card as a rightful part of every situation. Death does mean change, and bidding farewell to the familiar can be painful. On a psychological level, the death of old habits or patterns can cause acute anxiety, as these are broken up to make way for the new. It is also possible to be addicted to change for its own sake, and so the card could be a warning not to be ruled simply by the desire to destroy the old and make a new start.

14. Temperance

Temperance is one of the most beautiful, soothing cards in the Tarot pack; the winged figure is indeed a Triumph of gentle control over flowing waters.[42] However, she has a rainbow spectrum of possible meanings, rather like a prism of light shining in the spray of the waters, created as she pours them endlessly. The waters do indeed seem to flow eternally in both directions, a form of superior recycling. One of her messages is that the resources we have will stay fresh and renew themselves if we use them moderately, but generously. Creating the right kind of flow is everything. Even the loveliest of Tarot images come with warnings, however, and in certain readings the card could indicate wastefulness, flux, or a vacillating instability.

This image goes back far in history: Temperance's action of pouring is similar to that of certain Assyrian deities, who were also shown in winged form, pouring out divine water into a receptacle. Although the Tarot card of Temperance is not likely to have a direct link with this mythology, it could link indirectly through the Renaissance emblematic use of Egyptian hieroglyphs, which followed on from Assyrian culture.[43] The winged figure also seems to suggest grace and a benign presence from another realm. The angelic dimension of existence seems to be recognized by people from different times and cultures. Many people have experienced the presence of angels, among them even those who are skeptical about religion or the existence of higher worlds. For any of us, the experience can remain a touchstone, reminding us of another order of being and a love and benevolence that transcend petty concerns. Although our conditioning may put particular forms upon this experience, the angel as a figure will always have a place in human reckoning, and the Tarot card can represent being touched by something higher. Perhaps this is symbolized by the gleam of otherworldly beauty in the five- or six-petaled flower of the Angel's headdress.

In terms of cultural history, Temperance represents one of the four cardinal virtues,[44] so in a simplistic interpretation it could be taken as a stern warning against drinking too much alcohol. But this is not the root of its meaning; earlier associated uses of the word include "temperament," meaning the blending of four elements to make up a person's type.[45] The waters mix in our own personalities, too; our energies and outpourings can be tempered by judicious mixing of our own emotions and reactions. Temperance in a Tarot reading may raise the question of balance and flow: are the energies flowing well, and are they being channeled correctly in a particular situation?

Winged Temperance was also called the Angel of Time (the words *time* and *temperance* are connected through their Latin roots), whose swiftly beating wings may announce the fleeting passage of time in human life. In a reading, the card could therefore raise the question of making good use of the time available to complete a project or simply live well.

15. The Devil

The Devil in this pack is a grotesque creature. The image we have here is apparently a stock type of devil, which originated with the Persians and Egyptians, reaching us via Byzantine art. Some Tarot card designers (as is evident in the Rider-Waite pack) have decided to make him more majestically horrible, a serious force of evil, instead of this squat, hairy creature. The Marseilles version of the Devil seems androgynous, with a female chest but male genitals, and he is also part beast and part bat with his claws, branching horns, and leathern wings. Sometimes he has gaping mouths depicted on his chest or stomach. Curiously enough, in Northern Italy at the same time as the Tarot emerged, similar images were used to portray "monstrous births" occurring in the population; this tells us that, however far-fetched these pictures were in terms of portraying babies with birth defects, there was a genuine horror of anything half-human. The Devil, then, might also indicate that danger of losing our humanity and sinking into a bestial state.[46]

Perhaps we should stay with the traditional Tarot Trump of a stupid, comic type of devil, rather than giving him glamorous satanic powers. One of the ways to reduce the power of the Devil has always been to mock him, as is celebrated in various folk songs and tales.[47] Although he is a monster, he is also ridiculous. The medieval monks, who carried on the story of the Devil in their magnificent illuminations, frequently chose to depict their devils and demons engaged in absurd antics. To laugh at the Devil can be a way of cutting him down to size, whereas a devil ignored or blindly attacked can grow into enormous proportions.

We don't use the term "devil" very much anymore. Perhaps terms like "bad habits," "negative emotions," and "obsession" have more meaning. But let's not assume that the Devil Trump has lost all his significance. Although the Devil in a reading does not for the most part represent evil, it can certainly indicate people or situations that are diminishing our capacity to act, think, or feel. The two little devils chained to his plinth have no apparent means of escape. Awareness of bondage is the first step: in human terms, to have a chance of becoming free, we first need to recognize that we are enslaved. Intelligence, compassion, or even cunning might be needed to release the ties that bind and to move on.

However, sometimes the Devil indicates that this is a situation of very limited choice. Doing what must be done can be another way of dealing with a difficult situation; it may be time to blow the whistle, file for bankruptcy, or get the police involved. Unpleasant choices must be made; the Devil must be faced. And the Devil shows us that with every choice and every acquisition come burdens and ties. "One house, one worry. Two houses, two worries," said the father of a Turkish family, whose summer house I was staying in, across the Bosphorus from their winter residence in Istanbul. "Take what you want, and pay the price" is another saying: the Devil is a reminder of the bill that must be paid.

16. The Tower

Lightning strikes the tower with a tongue of fire; the walls are breached, men fall from the heights, and stones rattle down to the ground. The scene is clear, and the message is plain: building high brings exposure to danger. Pride comes before a fall. All that seemed safe and secure can be demolished in an instant.

In our daily world, external danger can come from both natural and man-made forces, whether it's earthquakes or faulty electric wiring. Risk can never entirely be ruled out, and there are many ways in which we can suddenly be struck or cast to the ground. But in a reading, this Tarot card is less likely to represent an external accident and is more likely to signify a rupture in the fabric of life, such as the abrupt end of a relationship, unexpected news, or a sudden change of residence. And in keeping with the rounded nature of Tarot symbols, we have to look at the image from different angles; shock and loss of some kind may well be involved, but perhaps this could be a liberating event. The change might also signify a happy release from an imprisoning situation. The essential point to grasp about the Tower, therefore, is that although it could suggest accident or misfortune, it is more likely to indicate a sudden or irrevocable point in the affairs of everyday life.

For a person who has been trapped, the Tower can reveal an end to that particular constraint, whether it is a stultifying relationship, a rigid set of rules at work, or a binding contract that restricts all other possibilities. We build towers as bastions, hoping that they will fix our position permanently; but if we ignore the signs that they have served out their purpose, the collapse of the structure can be painful. The impact may be hard, but the change opens the door to freedom and new possibilities.

In a rounded reading, we can try to see too what aspect of the Tower predominates. As mentioned at the start of this chapter, the general theme of the question, the position of the Tower within the spread, and its relationship to the other cards around it can help to highlight one element over another. So, for instance, the unexpected strike of lightning could be the main factor, indicating a sudden "bolt out of the blue." Or perhaps the stones that fall from the sky are the key feature, signifying loss of money, status, or possessions.

Historically, the Tower concurs with medieval illustrations of the vice of pride.[48] As Nicola McDonald points out in her book *Pulp Fictions of Medieval England*, "A fall from a tower became precisely the emblem of divine retribution for arrogant faithlessness in the later Middle Ages."[49] This harks back to the story of the Tower of Babel in the Bible, where men tried to build a tower reaching up to heaven, only to have their edifice shattered by God as punishment for their impudence and pride. Then, the story goes, men began to speak in a multitude of languages, instead of just one tongue. So, in a way, the myth suggests that a kind of creative linguistic and cultural diversity was a consequence of destroying the tower, which offers us yet another positive side to the meaning of the fall from the Tarot Tower.

Lightning, the active dynamic of the Tarot image, looms large in traditional lore. It is often perceived as a sign of God's wrath and is held in fearful awe even in modern times, not only for the damage it causes, but for its significance as a mark of divine intervention. The lightning strike on the Anglican cathedral of York Minster in 1984, three days after the consecration of a controversial bishop, was seen by many as an angry message.[50] And there are many records of towers being hit by lightning over the centuries, catastrophic events for the most part, which were marveled over as omens and branded as the work of either God or the Devil. The most prominent examples include accounts of lightning strikes on parish churches in Europe[51] and the medieval "skyscraper" towers in Northern Italy.[52] It's easy to see how the mythology of the Tower struck by lightning became rooted in popular imagination and also became a symbol of separating right from wrong: those who were spared by the lightning flash could be considered righteous, while those who were damaged by it were often branded as wrongdoers. The tower may therefore stand as a warning to sort out our lives and make firm, even ruthless decisions about what should remain and what should be cast aside.

The Tower struck by lightning can indeed mean havoc or a sudden change, but as usual with Tarot symbols, the interpretation can flow only when we ask further questions: How does this change work for the person or situation concerned? What may be lost here? What may be gained? What are the new possibilities opening up?

17. The Star

The Star is akin to Temperance in that an angel in the former and a naked girl in the latter pour water from two jugs. But here the water is poured out, one jug pouring into the waters of what could be a river or lake, while the other pours water onto the ground. This is a card where nothing is kept back. Nakedness, openness, and giving forth characterize the figure of the Star. She can be interpreted as hope, generosity, and healing. Perhaps she is also a sign of female beauty and sexuality. But the actual name of the card is the Star, so the naked girl herself is most probably an emblem of the biggest and brightest star shown in the constellation of (usually) seven other stars. I think her nakedness is more a symbol of the soul than of sexuality; stars were often believed to be souls that had migrated from human life to the heavens, and the bird on the tree usually symbolizes a messenger from the world of souls. Looking at the Star in this way, we come to a sense of transcendent beauty rather than an earthly one, and to a sign that the flow of life connects this world with celestial spirit. There is much to be pondered here.

It's possible that this card could also be a sign of initiation, especially within the general context of myth and tradition. Although I can't vouch for any historical connection, the collection of myths surrounding the associated goddesses Ishtar from Babylonia and Anahita from Iran carry a startling likeness to the Star. Ishtar is often symbolized as the Morning Star and is sometimes known as the Star of Lamentation; Anahita is the goddess of the heavenly waters that flow from the region of Venus among the stars. In one of the key myths, Ishtar decides to travel to the center of the underworld to fetch the water of life to restore her dead lover, Tammuz, god of the harvest. She passes through seven gateways, leaving behind one of her jeweled adornments at each portal, until she arrives naked at the sacred pool. Here, in this underworld, the souls of the dead are represented by birds.[53] This is at the very least a compelling parallel to the scene shown on the Star of the Tarot. Taking this back into the realm of a contemporary Tarot reading, the Star may therefore indicate an inner journey, as opposed to the Chariot, which more often signifies outer forms of travel.

Bringing this back to everyday life, I suggest that the Star may symbolize the heart of the matter, the point at which there is no further secrecy or pretense. Here, resistance and defensiveness are dissolved. There is giving and receiving through the outpouring of living water. As with Temperance, this could also be taken as a sign of grace or blessings to be received. But whereas with Temperance the energies are always kept in balance and moderation is the key to a happy flow, here the Star gives all she has, without stinting. In a less propitious sense, this could also mean giving too much in a way that might not benefit the donor or the receiver. If one person is trying to help another, it suggests too that the situation may be delicate and has to be handled carefully. It can be a card of empathy, but, in excess, it could denote a lack of discretion through the tendency to "pour everything out." Overall, however, the Star is a symbol of brave generosity.

18. The Moon

The Moon as a Tarot Triumph embodies the world of emotion, dreams, and imagination. Who can gaze at this card and not feel the stirring of something being drawn up from the depths? The power of the moon over the waters may not be altogether comfortable, though; it can disturb balance and compromise our sense of safety. It is a shifting presence that can change moods and fancies and create difficult physical sensations too, such as restlessness, nervous excitement, and broken sleep patterns. It draws the tides of the body whether we wish it to or not. A prominent Moon in a reading, in an appropriate position, could indicate that the body is in a delicate condition and that rest and sleep are needed to settle the metabolism.

The Moon brings rich gifts from the imagination, to be used with care. As a Tarot card, the Moon can also represent psychic phenomena, such as premonitions and intuitions. Perhaps the towers in the image indicate the threshold between the earthly world and the otherworld, which can indeed be seen as the boundary between normal and supernatural perception but also, on occasion, as the line between reality and illusion.[54] In a reading, this card might therefore suggest the need to check out the truth of a situation and watch out for deception. It could also indicate a positive upsurge of creativity as an inventive or artistic idea takes shape in the imagination.

The moon is personified as a god or goddess in just about every culture, but it is difficult to pin down this particular form of the image to exact sources. In the Marseilles Tarot, the Moon always has a face, but one which may be shown either straight on or in profile, so this gives no clues.[55] The dogs could be the hunting dogs of the classical moon goddess Diana, but they are also reminiscent of the dog and scorpion (similar to the crayfish) that are portrayed in the initiatory symbols of Mithraism, the Roman mystery religion, where they are depicted alongside images of the heavenly bodies. They might also, more simply, represent dogs baying at the moon, although even further back, certain Babylonian boundary stones show a crescent moon associated with towers, doglike animals, and a crayfish or scorpion.[56] This may not connect directly to the Tarot, but it does underpin the importance of a moon motif associated with symbols of a threshold and creatures of the deep.[57] Finally, the drops that fall from the sky could be the sacred dew that is important in both alchemy and mystical Kabbalah.[58] Dew also falls from the Great Head of Macroprosopus in the mystical traditions of Kabbalah. I think we have to go with the appropriately watery "swim" of correspondences here, allowing them to influence our interpretation of the Moon without being too concerned about the exact sources. Wherever it originates, the Moon continues to fascinate generations of Tarot users.

19. The Sun

Unlike the complex, elusive Moon, the Sun shines forth in its simplicity. Its qualities are truth, openness, warmth, and generosity; it could also indicate friendship in a reading, along with trust and personal integrity. Thus, the Sun in a prominent position may denote new energy and growth or the healing of a rift. All in all, it speaks of creativity, love, and joy. Every Triumph has its downside, though, and the Sun can also signify excessively high spirits, reckless enthusiasm, or overindulgence in pleasure.

From the historical Tarot cards that survive, we can see that the Sun, like the Moon, settled into one chief representation three or four hundred years ago after appearing in a few variations, such as that of a naked boy holding the sun, or, more notably, riding a horse and carrying a banner, which may represent the Sun as Victory in Christian terms.[59] Another version shows a woman spinning thread under the Sun's rays, an action that is associated with fate and time, and thus probably indicating the importance of the sun as cosmic timekeeper and ruler of the seasons for our life on earth.[60] The sun as governor of life cycles is certainly an aspect to keep in mind. The Marseilles version shows two identical semi-naked boys linking arms in kinship or friendship as the "drops" of the sun fall around them. We can interpret the drops in the same way as for the moon, but what do the boys themselves mean?

One link may be with the twins in the zodiac sign of Gemini, the sign whose end marks the summer solstice in June and the time when the sun is at the height of its powers in the Northern Hemisphere. The twins have been a zodiac emblem since at least 1000 BCE, the formative period of Babylonian astrology, and, given the prevalence of astrology in the late medieval period, when the cards were first used, this would be a natural correspondence to make. But the twins may have earlier origins and a more widespread application; male twins have been associated with the sun from at least as early as the Bronze Age, where various pictures show them holding axes alongside images of the sun. This connection between twins and the sun is thought to have carried on right through the Roman era up until the nineteenth century, according to various European folk customs recorded then.[61] Depictions during this long period include the twins Castor and Pollux in classical mythology, twin figures in Mithraism holding flaming torches that represent the rising and setting sun, and twin males kindling new fire in the sun rituals of folk tradition.

This gives us a surprising number of references to twins and the sun, but no firm indication as to which the Tarot makers chose. Perhaps it is better, as with the Moon, to keep all these allusions in mind but to focus primarily on contemplating the pleasing, warming simplicity of little children playing in the life-giving light of the sun. Here, too, there is a "boundary," a wall behind the boys. So perhaps this also stands as a marker between the worlds.[62] The Sun is our benefactor, but there will always be a division between our earthly world and the heavens.

20. Judgment

The image of the Last Judgment is well known in Christian iconography and does not need much additional explanation in terms of its historical connotations. The Angel summons the "sleepers," those who have died, to wake up from their graves and face their maker to be judged as to whether they have done good or evil in their earthly lives.[63] The trumpet sounds, and the dead thus awaken to face judgment. However, we can extend the field beyond specifically Christian beliefs and call it an *awakening* rather than judgment as such, since the scene is of that trumpet call to awakening rather than the weighing of souls.

Spiritual wake-up calls are embedded in other teachings too. A moving example is found in the Gnostic text *The Hymn of the Robe of Glory*, an allegory of man's divine origins and an assertion that life here on earth is spent in exile until we wake up to our true inheritance. Here, the King's son has left the heavenly palace and descended into "Egypt," the realms of material life on earth. He sleeps and is in danger of forgetting everything he once knew. But his royal parents send him a message: an eagle is dispatched with a letter from the celestial land:

> Up and arise from thy sleep,
> Give ear to the words of Our Letter!
> "Remember that thou art a King's son; . . .
> Remember thy Glorious Robe, . . .[64]

Coming forward to the current era, the twentieth-century spiritual teacher George Gurdjieff also put great emphasis on the need to wake up and realize that human beings are asleep for most of the time.[65]

So, in the context of the Tarot Triumphs, this card shows a stirring and quickening of life. What seemed to be dead is shown to live; what has died is reborn, or is about to be reborn in another form. We can apply this trumpet call in a reading to anything from a phone call from an old friend, to an unexpected job opportunity, or indeed a powerful realization that it's time to wake up to the real meaning of life. It could indicate an impulse arising, a message, or a surprise.

Although I have suggested that waking up is the main focus of the card, nevertheless Judgment does imply another layer of significance. Whereas Death suggests the end of a phase, a life, a relationship, or whatever else, Judgment points to what comes afterward. Death hints at new life ahead, but Judgment takes us into the realm of accountability and understanding. After the first awakening come trials and tests. Can the old friendship survive in a new phase of life? How demanding is this new job? What ordeals and possible sacrifices must be faced in order to achieve true inner transformation? The trumpet of the angel promises new life, but the judgment of truth too.

21. The World

The World turns; the tread of the dancer keeps the eternal movement going, while at the four fixed corners the holy creatures watch the dance of life revolve.

When I first began researching the origins of Tarot imagery many years ago, I was astonished to find that this image of a turning world appeared in medieval art in a form known as "Christ in Glory," or "Majesty," as it is commonly entitled. But instead of the dancer, as depicted here, it shows Christ enthroned at the center of the world. Both versions, however, are surrounded by the symbols of the Four Evangelists: ox, lion, eagle, and angel.[66] The Tarot Triumph seemed an audacious substitution, especially since the dancer is a naked young woman draped only with a flimsy scarf, which if anything heightens her charms rather than covers them. However, there is another way of looking at this, I discovered. This Tarot image could have been perceived, in Renaissance times especially, as the *anima mundi*, or the world soul. This is a way in which Neoplatonic teachings could be understood within the Christian framework of the time, and an image that combined the two might have been acceptable even to more conventional minds.

The concept of a "world soul" was apparently first formulated by Plato in the Timaeus[67] and was also embodied in mystical teachings from the early centuries CE, such as the kabbalistic and hermetic philosophies.[68] In Kabbalah, it is personified as Shekinah, the feminine grace of God as it descends to the garden of creation, and is there symbolized by the beauty of woman. Perhaps it also accords with the representation of the sacred force of nature in alchemy. Other early versions of this card may also back up the notion that she was no ordinary dancing girl, but a representation of holy truths; the main coun-terparts, alternatives for the Triumph of the World, were images of the Holy City Jerusalem and the Holy Grail.

These three images help to affirm the nature of the World as a symbol. The dancing girl in her spiritual show-case, the city that represents heaven on earth, and the chalice that is the ultimate spiritual object all symbolize the presence of the Divine in earthly form. This form is material, yet it is sacred. It may be attainable, we are told, after long struggles that might involve both an inner and an outer journey. The symbol of the Triumph can there-fore be seen as the human quest itself, and it indicates the sacredness of the world around us.

In the world soul we have a fitting ending to the series of twenty-two Trumps, announced by the Fool and led in by the Magician. But here, as with all the Triumphs, there are questions we can ask in order to shed light on the meaning of the symbol. What music does the lady dance to? Perhaps it is the Music of the Spheres, which emanates from the angelic realms. Or perhaps it is a less worthy tune; the World could in a reading represent someone who is too caught up in the rhythm of worldly values and the frothy tunes of fashion. But it might also signify a person or situation where there is real harmony and contentment. The rhythm may be steady and satis-fying, and the melody one that continually refreshes the senses. Sometimes drawing the World in a reading can indicate that everything is going along as it should and that it is unnecessary to disturb the balance.

Here then is a card that can symbolize fulfillment as well as remind us of the bigger picture of life and give us a sense that our lives are forever in motion. Divina-tion oracles such as the Tarot are based on the principle of change[69] and on cycles and revolutions of time. The concept of a cycle within which the dancer treads her steps is shown here as the wreath or mandorla that surrounds her.[70]

But even if *anima mundi*, or the world soul, acts as a good label for this card, we will miss something unless we return to the implied juxtaposition of the two figures who can both lay claim to their place within this image: the dancing girl and Christ. It brings a final opportunity in the sequence of Tarot Triumphs to grasp the paradox and find yet more avenues to explore in understanding the symbol. In this light, I suggest that the World as Tarot Triumph is both male and female, sacred and secular, and that it marries elements from opposite poles of experience. All the strife between different forces—think back to the Lover and his choice, and the cruel rotation of the Wheel of Fortune—is resolved here. There is reconciliation and integration of energies and values. As the last numbered card in the pack, it therefore indicates union and completeness. The spiritual world and the material world are conjoined, and the World can thus remind us of the beauty to be found in the commonplace.

Chapter Six

A SEARCH FOR ORDER AND MEANING IN THE FOOL'S MIRROR

After pondering each Tarot image, the questions arise, How are they all connected? Is there meaning in the ordering of the cards? This is a legitimate line of inquiry, but there is plenty of scope for debate, and no one final answer.

The first section of this chapter considers possible ways of defining the Tarot sequence, highlighting one in particular but also emphasizing the need for a flexible approach when interpreting the patterns of Tarot numbering. In the second section, we move on to tackle a new Tarot spread—the Celtic Cross—where the layout encompasses a sense of ordering through its cross formation. At this point, the positions of the cards in a reading begin to have their own significance. This relatively straightforward but effective Tarot spread is very handy to use for divination. It also acts as a stepping-stone between the three-card reading and the full Fool's Mirror layout.

TAROT NUMBERING

The numbering in the Marseilles-type traditional pack is consistent, starting with the Magician as no. 1, ending with the World as no. 21, and designating the Fool as either unnumbered or 0. But this was not so in the earliest packs that remain; numbering in the first fifty years or more of recorded Tarot examples was either nonexistent or inconsistent. In certain packs, too, some of the cards were numbered, while others were not. So we can't rely on an original, historic number sequence to point the way to the intentions of the earliest Tarot makers. However, since the numbering in the Marseilles version did settle down into the sequence that we now know, from the early sixteenth century onward, it seems that those who designed and used the cards were by that time content with the order, whether they understood this to have an implicit meaning or not.

Even though the numbering took the best part of a century to gel, this does not rule out the significance of Tarot numbering in itself. Meaning within a system is not necessarily fixed right from the start. In the same way that astrology took centuries to develop into the form that we recognize today, Tarot too may have gradually evolved toward its optimum form.[1] Just as the images of the Tarot Triumphs took time to crystallize, so a number sequence might have been cooking for a while. Perhaps a person or persons unknown played a conscious role in embedding a complete symbolic and numerical framework within the deck, or perhaps its usage over time, including the playing of the game Tarocchi, finally settled the Trumps into a convenient form shaped by popular imagination into a satisfying and meaningful deck. Some form of evolution has certainly taken place, and further historical research may in time reveal more about this process; but for the moment, our starting point for investigation stands as the existing numbered sequence of the twenty-two Triumphs.

Number and pattern form a part of most symbolic systems. The concept that certain geometric forms and certain numbers are both important and sacred is found at the heart of many philosophical, mystical, and religious teachings.[2] So it naturally follows that we will seek for this within the Tarot too, and many people indeed do choose to hunt for implicit significance within the Tarot numbering. After all, twenty-two (or twenty-one plus one) is an interesting number to investigate—it is less common as a symbolic number than, say, seven, ten, or twelve, but with some potentially strong associations. The two most prominent are the correspondence with the twenty-two letters of the Hebrew alphabet, which in turn accord with the twenty-two paths on the kabbalistic Tree of Life, and the mathematical principle that there are twenty-one different throws achievable with two dice, the dice we can indeed see in many representations of the Magician, Trump no. 1.[3]

There seems to be a trail to follow here, but there is no agreed way of analyzing this with Tarot, and no certain way to discern any original intention in the numerical design of the pack for the historical reasons just mentioned. Some might argue that we should instead be looking at the number seventy-eight, in packs that include both the Tarot Triumphs and the four suits of fourteen cards each.[4] But the Trumps can rightfully be thought of as a separate entity, as they were created separately and often used independently. The Trumps stand as a series of picture symbols in their own right, and even where they are used in conjunction with the four suits in divination and games, they have always been accorded higher value. The suits, with their emphasis on number and court cards, do not carry the same weight and significance.[5]

TAROT TRIUMPHS AS THREE SETS OF SEVEN

I offer in this chapter one straightforward way of dividing up the twenty-two Triumphs as three sets of seven plus one. You may remember the encounter with Raz, one of my three Tarot masters, which I described in the first chapter. He introduced me to this notion that the twenty-one numbered cards can be seen as three sets of seven, in this case following each other in sequence, as in a large circle. The three sets thus form three segments of this circle, each with its own qualities, but together making one complete cycle. The Fool presides at the center of the circle.

The first series of seven comprises the Magician, the High Priestess, the Empress, the Emperor, the Pope, the Lover, and the Chariot. They can be seen as cards of *being*. We can become any one of those characters and take on their roles. They have the simplicity of intention and a personal power that equates with basic human drives.

The second series contains Justice, the Hermit, the Wheel of Fortune, Strength, the Hanged Man, Death, and Temperance. These can be interpreted as cards of *interaction*; the emphasis is on how we respond to the world and external forces, how we balance their energies and adjust to their demands. All these cards represent a choice, a way in which we can act in handling situations.

The third series consists of the Devil, the Tower, the Star, the Moon, the Sun, Judgment, and the World. Here, the emphasis seems to shift to external forces that affect us. These may be cards of *higher energy* that come from a different realm; note that the sky is a prominent feature in these cards, with the exception of the Devil, whose world anyway has no sky as we know it.

In this interpretation, then, the first series is the most personal, the second encompasses our dealings with the world and our fellow human beings, and the third denotes events and forces emanating from another level. This analysis is not the sole possible interpretation, but it may serve as a useful guide to seeing some kind of progression through the pack, with three marked stages and a consistency of imagery within each set of seven.

EXERCISES

These are brief exercises suggested in order to get an impression of the differences between these three sets, and of the way in which the cards belong there. Any impressions gained need not dominate your interpretation but may act as a useful point of reference. Keep notes if you wish.

Exercise One: Cards of Being

Identify three key character traits of each card in this first set. Keep to this number even if you think there could be more. For instance, I might see those of the Chariot as "drive," "determination," and "control." You might come up with "will," "energy," and "skill." Just choose those you find useful, and then see them form a dynamic that determines the nature of the figure on the card. How does the character act and behave in accordance with that dynamic?

Exercise Two: Cards of Interaction

What is the main interactive function of each of these cards? With what dynamic do they operate, and to what end? Try to describe this with just one phrase or sentence to bring clarity to the meaning of the card's position within this set of seven. For instance, the rotation of the Wheel of Fortune could suggest, "From the inevitable cycles of good and bad fortune, we can learn both how to seize opportunity and how to let go at the right moment." Temperance could mean, "It is important to use the right sort of vessels to contain the flow of energy and to moderate the flow so that nothing is wasted unnecessarily."

Exercise Three: Cards of Higher Energy

How do you see these higher energies working? How might they affect a person? Find a phrase or sentence to encapsulate the meaning. For example, for Judgment, "There is a force in the universe that can awaken us to new life even when everything seems to be inert."

OTHER OPTIONS

For our purposes, it is better to build a foundation for Tarot practice using just one or two number concepts. However, for anyone who would like to penetrate further into the mathematical significance of Tarot numbering, there are other ways of cutting up the cake: you may choose to focus on the Tarot as two sets of eleven cards, or as sets of ten and twelve. We can also investigate the interface between twenty-one and twenty-two, or consider the relationship between six and twenty-one, since six steps of addition bring us to that sum: $1 + 2 + 3 + 4 + 5 + 6 = 21$.

There is no restriction on combining these perspectives, either, so a more elaborate philosophical interpretation of the Tarot could be constructed around a combination of the different ways of analyzing the number sequences.

Three Circles

A further way of distributing three sets of seven is to picture them as three circles that overlap, thus creating one fully overlapping segment at the center. This is not such an easy shape to place the cards in physically, but it is an elegant and more abstract form for contemplation. It throws up certain questions for consideration, such as how to arrange the cards in each circle, and where on the circumference of each circle the starting cards for each sequence (nos. 1, 8, and 15) would be placed.

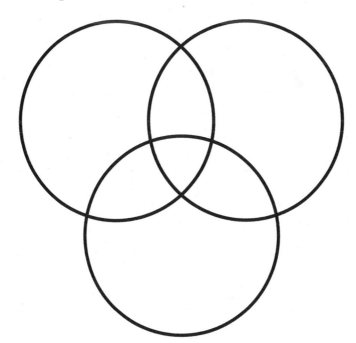

I open this up for your consideration, and although I have not done the further investigation myself, it holds promise as a future line of research.[6] It could even become, in a modified form, a layout for Tarot divination, with a shuffled pack: the three circles could signify different spheres of life and special significance could be accorded to the cards that fall on the overlapping segments. (See chapter nine for other suggestions for creative development with Tarot.) This will present further challenges on how to make the physical form of the layout work, but it just goes to show that there is exciting territory to explore. The attempt to identify number sequences and geometric forms within the Tarot can lead to further discoveries and new applications of the cards.

Storytelling

Although, in my view, the circle is the most natural way of envisaging the Tarot sequence, we could also see it in a linear way, as if telling a story. Earlier, we tried out the storytelling potential of Tarot, and although extending this from three cards to twenty-two might need a real stretch of the imagination, it is perfectly possible to give it a go.

For this, lay out the cards in their numerical order, starting with the Fool, and try to see what kind of narrative is unfolding from the Magician at no. 1 to the World at no. 21. It's possible too to try this in reverse order from no. 21 to no. 1. I suggest that you approach this in a spirit of play and enjoyment without forcing the story to take its full shape. You may also find that this exercise is worth coming back to a few times; it will probably grow easier and more enjoyable as you practice.

Another idea would be to work on stories that are only seven cards long, but by taking sequences of seven that do not correspond with the sevenfold numbering template that I've just described. For instance, your story could run from the Empress to the Hermit, or the Hanged Man to the Moon. As well as being creative and, hopefully, enjoyable, this will help to give an idea of how the sequence of the Tarot cards develops within the complete pack.

The Ladder

Another way of looking at the sequence of twenty-two cards is to envisage it as a ladder of spiritual progress or evolution, with each successive Tarot card taking its place on the next rung up. The numbering could run in either direction. It could be seen as beginning with the Fool or the Magician at the bottom, standing for the individual human soul in its initial state, and arriving at the top rung with card no. 21, the World, symbolizing the completion of the pilgrimage. But there is also a good case for reversing it, with the World representing the earthly state where we start our journey and the Magician as the most exalted state of being, where the individual has become an adept at working with the forces of creation. The Fool here is still something of a wild card; he could be at the bottom or the top—or perhaps he is able to participate at any point on the ladder.

Although I mention this possibility of spiritual ascent in connection with the Tarot, I hesitate to do so, because I think it is more productive to think of the Tarot as a sequence of symbols that are all equal in status, with each one comprising both spiritual and mundane levels. If you wish to use Tarot as a system for spiritual development, or to align it with another spiritual ladder–type tradition, like the kabbalistic Tree of Life, then you may indeed want to interpret it as hierarchical in this sense.

But for divination, where we must keep a degree of fluidity, this is too rigid a concept.

Looking at this another way, if we tie ourselves firmly to one particular sequential meaning of the numbering, then we may end up limiting the attributions of the cards themselves. Say, for instance, that I consider the World to be the crowning glory of the pack as the highest number (21) and imagine that it always represents completion and a major attainment. That means that in a Tarot reading I won't be open to other possible interpretations, such as an emphasis on the mundane rhythm of everyday existence, or the benefit of worldly practicality in a particular situation. We need to allow our intuition to come into play within the scope of a Tarot divination. If there is too fixed an interpretation, then we lose many of the possibilities that the cards inherently possess.

THE LAUGHTER OF THE FOOL

It can be hard to place the Fool definitively in any of these sequences and constructs. Perhaps the Fool may have the last laugh after all if he stands outside the numbering, knowing that there is in fact no intended number symbolism within the pack. He may watch us all struggling to make sense of the sequence and smile at our folly. But he also knows that we will gain from this, that the effort will sharpen our wits, make us appreciate the strength of the Tarot images, and lead us on to trying out new ways of interpreting them. The Fool is there to stop us from taking everything for granted. Maybe individual numbering was never meant to matter much if the cards were intended to be fluid and to be shuffled into different orderings and combinations. Even the game Tarocchi is not in one fixed form and has many different sets of rules. There might always have been an intention that we could approach the patterning of the Tarot in different ways so that it becomes a kind of universal picture book, open to interpretation from different viewpoints and in different contexts.

Although this can be frustrating, this elusiveness is part of the fascination of the Tarot. It also bestows freedom, allowing us to consider different interpretations of the number sequence. If we do choose to adopt one preferred and particular set of meanings for the ordering, then the best thing is to regard that set as a kind of blueprint in the static pack; but in a reading we should envisage the Triumphs as fluid, flexible, and capable of combining in a multitude of ways.

THE SIMPLE CELTIC CROSS LAYOUT

Now we move on to a new layout for Tarot reading, one that takes us from using three or four cards to a spread involving seven cards from the Tarot Triumphs. As well as being a useful Tarot layout in its own right, it offers practice in reading from a larger number of cards, preparing the way for the Fool's Mirror spread in the next chapter, which uses all twenty-two Trumps. And as a structured layout, with each card placed in order in a designated position, it chimes in with the general theme of pattern and sequence in this chapter.

The spread we are about to encounter is a simplified version of the popular Celtic Cross Tarot layout. Here, the cards are placed in order to make an equal-armed cross formation. Each position in the formation has its own specific significance, which helps to shape the meaning of the card placed there. The Celtic Cross also embodies a time sequence of past, present, and future. It thus moves us on from the fluid interplay of the three- and four-card readings to a more fixed and detailed structure for divination. However, it does bear a relationship to what we have covered previously, since there is a core triad of cards included in the layout that can certainly be considered in its own right.

A Note on the Layout

For each of the three main types of Tarot readings in this book—the three-card reading in chapter four, the seven-card Celtic Cross layout here, and the full Fool's Mirror layout using all twenty-two Trumps in chapter seven—I give a separate account of the process of laying out the cards. This is partly because there are slight variations for each layout, but also so that we can go further into the nuances of the reading method as we progress from a simple to a more complex type of spread. In the full exposition of the Fool's Mirror layout that follows this chapter, for instance, you will find more detailed instructions on how to begin and end the reading, and more debate about the ethics of Tarot reading in chapter eight. Once we have covered all three layouts, we reach a point too where we can vary the approach if we wish. Card reading is a form of ritual, and, as such, it needs structure; but the guidelines for this act as a template, not a straitjacket. They can be adapted to different circumstances. The important factor in the Fool's Mirror approach to divination is to have insight into why certain methods and practices are used; that way, we can alter them if appropriate.

Proceed with the Celtic Cross

Let's assume that you have someone who wishes to ask a question of the cards. First, ask that person to formulate a question and invite them to say what it is.

If you don't have a willing guinea pig and want to do a practice run anyway, then just read for yourself. But I strongly suggest that you keep the question to something relatively simple that does not have too much importance.

What Kind of Question?

The Celtic Cross layout can be used for a general "What is my situation?" type question, but it is better for a specific inquiry. It is a good layout for pinning things down, so the question can certainly be about practical matters—money, children, love, property, legal matters, work, health, education, friends, and business are typical of everyday issues that arise. Try to make sure that the question is properly defined, and encourage the person to refine the wording if necessary so that it is put clearly and succinctly. Tarot is robust, and an apparently mundane question will not devalue its deep symbolism. Remember too that Tarot has been used as a game and that its keynote is accessibility; people can bring their everyday concerns to it. And you may in any case find that the reading will reveal deeper, hidden elements to an apparently simple question.

But never neglect the obvious; there is also the converse risk that we can overlook what is staring us in the face and miss the main subject of the question altogether. The example I'm about to give comes from a fuller type of reading, but it serves to make a point about the importance of listening properly and not getting carried away with one's own ideas and inclinations.

This reading took place many years ago at a supper party that my former husband and I were hosting. Glyn, my Tarot teacher, was present, along with a friend of ours, a yoga teacher in her fifties named Janet. We all chatted through the evening, covering various fascinating topics ranging from our work and families to more spiritual and esoteric matters. Then Glyn offered to do a card reading for Janet. It was to be a general reading of her situation. Whatever he said plainly made sense to her, but I was puzzled by the way he interpreted the cards. After Janet left, I asked Glyn what it was all about.

"Well," he said. "Did you hear the *real* question of the evening?"

I shook my head. "I don't think so," I said. I assumed that he meant something really deep and ran through all the elevated themes we'd covered, but I couldn't come up with what I thought might be the right answer.

"It was about her child. Her daughter."

I had to accept that Glyn was right. Janet was a single parent deeply worried about her adolescent daughter. I *had* heard the implied question but had chosen to ignore it. I was keen to pursue exciting metaphysical ideas that evening and had screened out my friend's emotional distress about her child. Admittedly, I was not the one doing the reading, and the diviner sits in his or her unique position in relation to the cards, but nevertheless I had missed the obvious.

So listen to the question the person asks, but listen also for what might be the underlying question, which could turn up in another guise; be receptive to what the person says, and don't be tempted to elaborate on it. And remember that often our most urgent preoccupations are about family, work, and love, before considering more complicated possibilities. Let the cards then tell you what it's really all about.

The Celtic Cross Tarot Reading

Shortened form, with 7 cards

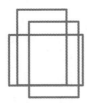

Significator (beneath)
1 (covering Significator)
2 (laid across Significator & 1)

The significator represents the person asking the
question and/or their situation.
No. 1 is the predominant feature of that situation
No. 2 is the challenge or obstacle facing the person
No. 3 is the goal or high point of the situation
No.4 is the basis of the situation
No. 5 is the recent past
No. 6 is the near future

Method

The querent formulates the question, speaks it out loud, and shuffles the cards.

As the reader, take the pack and spread it out in your hands, holding the backs toward the other person, and invite the querent to pick one card. You can gradually fan out sections of the cards in slow motion if that helps, rather than trying to spread them out all at once. Usually, the querent picks out the card quickly and decisively without further prompting.

Place this card faceup in what will be the center of the reading. It is the *significator*.

Put the pack back together without changing the order of the cards. Then invite the querent to cut the pack with the left hand, replacing the two halves after each cut so that the bottom half becomes the top half. Do this three times in all. If the querent is left-handed, ask them to use their right hand for this.

Then lay out the cards faceup as follows, drawing from the top of the pack while saying, or calling to mind, the words marking the placing of each card:

No. 1—Place the first card on top of the significator and say: "This covers you."

No. 2—Lay the following card across the significator: "This crosses you."

No. 3—Place above the significator: "This is above you."

No. 4—Place below the significator: "This is below you."

No. 5—Place to the left of the significator: "This is behind you."

No. 6—Place to the right of the significator: "This is before you."

You can speak these words out loud as you lay out the cards if you feel it is appropriate. Whether you think of it as a prayer, an incantation, or a practical road map of the reading, it can set the scene effectively. If you prefer to keep silent while placing the cards, then explain the positions of each card to the querent as you are giving the interpretation.

The layout now has seven cards in position: the significator plus the six cards that define the different elements of the situation.

Once the significator is placed on the table, you could choose to lay out the rest of the cards facedown and then turn them up one by one, speaking about each card as you reveal it. (The "covering" and "crossing" cards, nos. 1 and 2, would then need to be turned over together.) Revealing them in this way does create a stronger dramatic effect, but I prefer to see the complete reading before interpreting individual cards. Together, they make a whole, and although you are going to analyze each card separately as well, the overall layout does have its own unique identity to be assessed. Even though there is a strong emphasis on the individual meaning and position of the cards, they do still interact with each other.

Interpretation

The significator sums up the person who is asking the question and/or the situation inquired about. For instance, if the Hermit is the significator, then it might be interpreted by saying, "You are working very much on your own at the moment." It could also signify an independent outlook, a lonely phase of life, or a quest to reach the truth. The beauty and the terror of Tarot are that there is no one definitive version of how to interpret this! But you do not have to judge the significator straightaway; you can see how it lies in relation to the other cards. You may also find that it is in some way defined by the question asked. If it is about a failing relationship, for example, then the appropriate interpretation could be, "You will need to make your own decisions here."

Card no. 1, which "covers" the significator, represents the predominant force, mood, or environment that affects the person.

Card no. 2, which "crosses" the significator, reveals the obstacle or opposing force at work. We can reasonably assume that even in the happiest of circumstances there is some resistance to change, or a challenge that needs to be met, and this is what the card depicts.

The Triad—the significator, no. 1, and no. 2—stand at the core of the reading. You can study them as a triad, in the same way as we did in the last chapter, and see how the three symbols interact, keeping in mind here the significance of their particular positions. My recommendation is to do this later in the reading, though, once you've studied the whole seven-card spread. And if you pick up the three cards, do not forget the order in which they were laid out when you replace them on the table!

Card no. 3, at the top, reveals the highest forces, the best aims, or the overall idea or goal in the situation.

Card no. 4 is placed at the lowest point of the reading and represents the practical elements, or the foundation, on which the matter rests.

Card no. 5, to the left of the cross, indicates the past, particularly that aspect of the past most relevant to the question. This is usually the near past, but it could in some cases represent a longstanding factor or long-ago event that is especially influential in the current situation.

Card no. 6, to the right of the cross, shows the new influences that will come to bear on the situation. This is usually in the near future.

A Note on Card Positions

All these six cards relate to the significator and the question asked; they derive their particular meaning in this reading from those two things. The significator and the question define the reading: do not be tempted to go further and speculate about additional events or the querent's overall psychological makeup, for instance; stay with what you can see in the cards. Although it's necessary to rein in irrelevant conjecture, you'll find that you can gain more insights than you might have expected from this apparently simple but ordered layout.

The original Celtic cross motif,[7] as an ancient design, also includes a circle as well as a cross, and this is a helpful image to keep in mind since it implies the circular motion of time within the reading and the way that "above and below" are also a part of the situation. In this reading, the cards thus give a means of forming a coherent picture of the person, their situation, the elements at play, and the potential outcome. It is a very useful layout to have in your Tarot repertoire.

The Origin and Design of the Celtic Cross Reading

The main source for this layout is A. E. Waite's *The Pictorial Key to the Tarot*, first published in 1911. As mentioned earlier, Waite produced his own carefully composed set of Tarot cards, referred to as the Rider-Waite pack, which were painted by Pamela Colman Smith and include pictorial versions of the four suits.[8]

Waite calls the layout "an ancient Celtic method of divination," but he also states that it "has been used privately for many years past in England" and, to his knowledge, has never been published before. Its origins are not known with any certainty; it may well have associations with the Order of the Golden Dawn, who might have invented it as part of their magical system, or perhaps it was based on an old folk fortune-telling spread, using playing cards rather than Tarot cards.[9]

Waite's Celtic Cross layout includes four more cards, making it an eleven-card spread. I have reduced it in scale for our purposes, since the seven-card layout is a more effective stepping-stone from the three-card reading to the full spread of twenty-two Trumps for the Fool's Mirror layout. I think this shorter version also works better if you are using only the Tarot Trumps for a reading, without the four suits; eleven cards out of twenty-two possibilities is an awkward number—it's too many to make the actual appearance of any one card significant. But if you do want to expand your own Celtic Cross readings into the full layout, you can find details in Waite's book or easily track it down online.[10]

MOVING FORWARD

Layouts such as the Celtic Cross, which use only a selection of cards drawn from the Major Arcana, are a valuable resource. You will find plenty more examples of spreads in the Tarot literature and online, if you feel the need to try out others as well.[11] I've chosen this particular sequence of Tarot spreads here—the three-card reading, to a four-card reading, then to the sevenfold version of the Celtic Cross, and finally to the complete set of Triumphs in the Fool's Mirror spread—as a way to build expertise and also show how different layouts may have their own particular uses, from direct, brief readings to more subtle and complex ones. In the next chapter, we move on to the final layout, which uses all twenty-two Triumphs.

Chapter Seven

THE FOOL'S MIRROR LAYOUT

Since the start of this book, we've built up a sound working acquaintance with the Tarot. I've invited you to make a more profound engagement with the individual cards; you've considered the themes of order and pattern, and the benefits of taking a flexible view on these; and you've learned a few layouts for divination. Now it's time to open up the divination practice fully with the Fool's Mirror layout, which uses a complete spread of all twenty-two cards. In this chapter, the focus is on constructing and interpreting the Fool's Mirror spread. In chapter eight, we will move on to the more far-reaching considerations of giving a reading. Finally, chapter nine is devoted to creative ways of working with Tarot and exploring its symbolism further.

I suggest reading this entire chapter before starting to practice with the cards. It will make more sense to see the whole process of working with this particular layout first. Exercises will help you along the way, but these will be easier to follow after looking at all the guidance given.

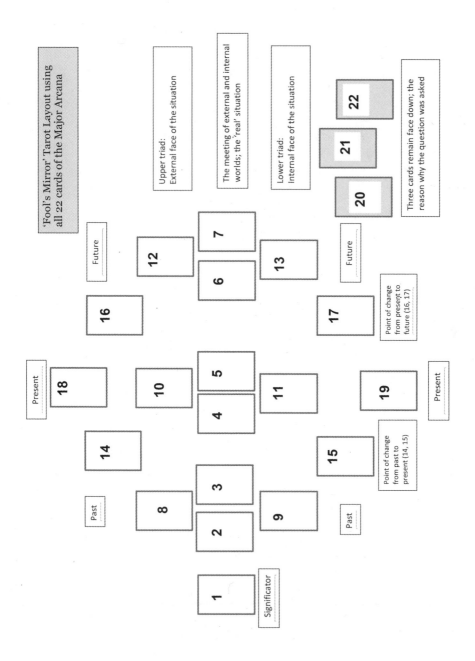

'Fool's Mirror' Tarot Layout using all 22 cards of the Major Arcana

Upper triad:
External face of the situation

The meeting of external and internal worlds; the 'real' situation

Lower triad:
Internal face of the situation

Three cards remain face down; the reason why the question was asked

Future

Future

Point of change from present to future (16, 17)

Present

Present

Point of change from past to present (14, 15)

Past

Past

Significator

A BRIEF GUIDE TO THE LAYOUT

On the diagram of the Tarot layout, the numbers represent the order in which the cards are laid out, and these numbers will be used in the text that follows to identify the different areas of the reading.

First of all, I'll go through the basic design and structure of the layout. Then, later, we will go into its inherent geometry and symmetry in more depth. Here are the key elements:

* The first card to be laid out is the significator, which represents either the person who asks the question or the subject of the question.

* The upper triangle represents the situation in the outer world: "real" events, other people, and external situations.

* The lower triangle represents what is happening in the inner world: personal feelings and forces working below the surface.

* The two halves reflect each other to some extent, but they have their own qualities too.

* The left-hand column of the reading represents the past, the central one the present, and the right-hand one the future.

* The central line is where inner and outer worlds interact, and each pair of cards placed there is a dynamic duo to be considered in combination.

* The six cards just above and below the center line (8–13) emphasize what is happening in the external and internal worlds.

* The transition points from past to present are marked by nos. 14 and 15, and the movement from present to

future are marked by nos. 16 and 17. These cards are the carriers of change.

✤ The uppermost and lowermost cards, 18 and 19, are the summit and the depth of the reading. They represent the culmination of external and internal forces respectively, but they are also indicators of how past, present, and future link together.

✤ The three cards laid facedown represent the reason why the question was asked. This is another way of saying, "What's missing from the situation?"

✤ The positions of the individual cards can be studied in detail, but the layout should also be read as a whole, as it is a "mirror" of the situation or person inquired about.

USING THESE DEFINITIONS

This is the key structure of the layout, and it's possible to do a reading just by grasping these principles. We can assimilate these basic definitions, and by adding in knowledge of the individual Tarot cards we may be able to deliver an interpretation of a full-card spread straightaway. However, in practice it can be challenging to plunge in so quickly, so what follows are exercises to help the acclimatization process. These exercises are followed by a consideration of the meanings of card positions in more depth, and then a more detailed guide to preparing and performing the reading.

EXERCISES

Before you approach a full card reading, I recommend doing a few practice exercises with the components of the layout. These are test runs and won't for the most part involve a real question, person, or situation, nor will they use the full spread of cards.

Note that the exercises don't follow the exact order in which you will lay out the cards for a full reading; they are designed to foster familiarity with the structure of the spread in the most effective way. As I mentioned, any references to the numbers of the card positions relate to the diagram, which shows the order of laying out the Tarot Trumps.

The Significator

We worked with a significator in the Celtic Cross layout, which represents the person asking the question or the matter inquired about, but it may be helpful to single it out further. Shuffle the pack, and spread it out either in your hand as a fan with the card backs toward you or facedown on a table in front of you. Pick out a card. Ask yourself two questions about the card:

✤ In a general reading, how does this card describe the person or their current situation?

✤ For a specific question, what might this card signify as the subject of the reading?

In most cases, you should be able to distinguish between these two possible types of answers, but bear in mind that there could also be an overlap.

Examples

I pick Temperance.

> As a person, this can represent someone who is concerned about balance in his or her life and is wondering what to do for the best. It is likely to have implications of giving, sympathy, and right use of energies.

As a question, it can relate to a matter of how to use resources wisely, including money. It could also be about the need for reconciliation or diplomacy.

I pick the Devil.

As a person, this can signify someone who is undergoing a great trial and struggling against forces that constrain him or her. It could indicate a rigid habit pattern that the person cannot break out of.

As a question, it can imply a situation where one must break ties or pay for past actions in order to be free again.

I pick the Fool.

The Fool is very special as a significator.

As a person, this signifies someone who is really open to hearing what the reading has to say. In the Fool's Mirror layout, this is actually the best position for the Fool to be in. It does not imply folly, though it can imply innocence or a touch of naivety. But openness is the prevailing quality.

As a question, it might mean that there is no specific or formulated question as such, and the Tarot reader can, in this case, offer to switch the reading to a more general appraisal of the situation. It may then happen that the reading helps to tease out any underlying questions that the querent hasn't been able to formulate.

From these examples, which I drew at random (no cheating allowed!), you can see some of the key interpretations for particular cards in the role of significator. You may find other angles to add to these examples, since my interpretations do not necessarily cover all the possibilities. For this exercise, it's enough to do it for three or four cards at a time in one session. If you find this useful, you could then do it for the whole pack (no need to draw randomly if you decide to interpret every card). Spread this over several days, taking a few cards at a time, so that you can come to them fresh each time. If you do work through the complete pack, I suggest writing down your perceptions and keeping them for future reference. Although definitions should not be too fixed, it can be helpful to have certain core interpretations that you can turn to for support.

The Middle Line (2–7)

For the main body of the layout, we'll base the first exercise on the center line of the cards (2–7). Shuffle the cards and then lay out the top six of the pack as the middle line of the spread, starting with the two cards on the left-hand side, followed by the two in the middle, then the final two on the right. Ask yourself: how might these cards indicate past, present, and future? As we don't have a significator here, it is probably easiest with this exercise and those following to assume that it's a general reading for a person.

In my sample set, I have the Pope and Justice, then the Emperor and the Chariot, followed by the World and the Lover. Here is my suggested meaning:

In the recent past, the person has had to go through a stringent legal process, or one where heavy protocol and restrictions were incurred; he or she could act only according to the rules.

Now there is much more chance for self-command and setting the desired direction.

In the future, much will be stabilized, but there will also still be an important issue of choice to be made and responsibilities that will come from this.

There could be a variety of ways to interpret this sequence, so rather than trying to come up with a definition that covers all possibilities, settle for one that strikes you as appropriate. In a "real" reading, the significator and the other cards would help to pin down the most relevant interpretation.

The Top and Bottom Cards (18 and 19)

Replace the cards, shuffle again, and this time pick out just two cards to represent the top and bottom of the reading (18 and 19 on the diagram). Study these as a pair: What could they be saying about the essence of the reading? What are the ultimate factors affecting past, present, and future? Remember that we do not have the previous cards from the middle row here to guide us. You are picking two cards for a separate study.

I pick the Moon and Temperance.

> To my mind, this suggests that the whole situation is very fluid and a touch unstable. The person tends to be over-affected by passing influences. A reality check is needed to dispel illusions. Inner life, though, is better balanced, and taking the two cards together, there is a richly imaginative quality to the person's psyche.

The Upper and Lower Cards (8–13)

Again, put the previous cards back into the pack, shuffle, and deal out the six cards in their positions above and below the center line. This is a little harder to tackle, but remember that they represent the most obvious external and internal aspects of the situation. You are also looking for potential contrasts between outside and inside.

Let's take my random set:

Past: the Empress above, the Hermit below

Present: the Devil above, the Sun below

Future: Death above, the Chariot below

In the past, a role of caring and protecting others (the Empress) contrasted with great privacy in terms of personal feelings (the Hermit). At present, there is a difficult, painful challenge to meet in the outside world (the Devil), which threatens destruction, but actually self-confidence has grown greatly and happiness is still possible (the Sun). In the future, there will be an aftermath to deal with from the present situation, and it may take time before new growth appears (Death). Considerable inner strength may be needed to deal with it (the Chariot).

As before, we would be likely to gain much more detail and definition in the context of a full reading, where the significator and other cards would shape up the interpretation.

The Transitional Cards (14–17)

Transitional cards are hard to read as a set without having the indicators for past, present, and future, so I suggest that you simply pick four cards separately, without placing them in a joint layout, and think about the kind of role that each card could play in moving a situation forward. You can also consider the different effects that they might represent on the inner level, as opposed to the external world.

Rather than doing a random reading here, it's probably more helpful if I just give some deliberately chosen examples. For instance, the Tower could mean a sudden change, loss, or even an accident if placed in the upper half of the reading, or a dramatic shift of viewpoint from the internal perspective in the lower half. Other cards may not be so marked in their effects: the Fool as a transitional could simplify signify time to be moving on, without regret, and the Lover could mark the moment of putting a decision into practice, perhaps one that has been pending for a while. The Tarot Trump Strength might signify that change has or will come about through using effort in the right way, perhaps achieving good results through a more gentle approach.

We can afford to be a little less defined with these transitional cards, as they take their color more from the cards around them. Even though I have said that the Tower could indicate an accident or mishap, this could be on a very minor level. (Remember that the card will turn up in every reading, and there isn't always an accident involved in every situation.) For instance, it might turn out to be something like leaving a notebook behind on a train, which in itself isn't a grave event. But that loss could trigger a whole new string of events, perhaps even positive ones: the person might decide to throw away a lot of tired ideas and start all over again with a project.

The Three Missing Cards

This is very similar to studying a trio of cards in the three-card reading, except that here they represent the elements that are "missing" from the situation. It is rather like one of those sliding plastic puzzles from childhood where you move the squares around the frame to try to make a picture, and you can do that only because there is an empty square to move the other pieces into. If there were nothing missing, no empty spaces, then it would be hard to adjust our lives.

Here, start by interpreting each card separately.

I have picked the Magician, the Wheel of Fortune, and the Star.

The Magician indicates a perceived loss of creativity and perhaps of joy and fun in life.

The Wheel of Fortune shows that there is a sense of being stuck, of not going anywhere. The motion of the wheel is missing.

The Star can mean that the person is lacking emotional interaction or a chance to nurture others.

Looking at the cards together, they could signify that there is a need to be more active, to seek out opportunities for change, to be more playful, and perhaps to be more openly responsive to others as well. This will help to get the subject's own energies and good fortune going again.

Final Advice

Treat these position exercises as something of a game. They do not need to be too serious, and definitely not too rigid in their interpretation. But they are useful: the practice of seeing the cards in their positions will help with the general assimilation of the layout.

THE PICTURE IN THE FOOL'S MIRROR

Now that we have looked at the basic structure of the twenty-two-card spread, we can move toward a deeper grasp of its symbolism. This kind of knowledge is something to be built up over time, so I recommend that you consider what follows but come back to it at later times for further contemplation, as your experience with the Fool's Mirror layout grows. After this section, we return to the practical process of doing a reading, and then we'll consider how we may gaze more profoundly into the Fool's Mirror and perhaps connect with a greater source of knowledge.

THE TRIADS ABOVE AND BELOW

The diamond shape of the Fool's Mirror spread reflects the way in which "above and below" can manifest in terms of human experience. It is not so much a question of what is higher and what is lower here, in the cosmic sense, but more the mirroring of exterior and interior experiences, and showing how they relate to each other. Although the cards in each half of the diamond do not replicate each other, they nevertheless relate to each other. Sometimes, for instance, they reflect each other like subtle variations of the same thing. On other occasions, though, you may be faced with a marked contrast between the two halves, which could represent a very sharp division between what someone is doing (outer triad above) and what he or she is feeling (inner triad below). The image of the mirror here works more as a metaphor, since it can indicate juxtaposition rather than literal reflection, like seeing the contrast of light and shadow or the interaction of two complementary colors. The central line is the meeting point of external and internal forces, representing this continuous interplay between them.

Are the forces in the two triads in harmony, or do they clash? This is a useful question to pose when considering the reading overall. Even if they do conflict, keep in mind that they are still two halves of a whole. In a reading, this might mean that the diviner can help the querent to understand that two apparently irreconcilable aspects of his or her life are in fact related to one another; if the person can recognize this, then a whole new dynamic is possible.

Although we can allow a degree of fluidity in interpreting this layout, some elements remain fixed: in this case, the definition of these two triads does need to remain as interior and exterior. They can certainly be seen as representing above and below the surface, but not as higher and lower forces in the sense of a spiritual or material hierarchy. The triad above and the triad below are equal in importance; they reflect each other, and they relate to each other.

THE TRIADS TO THE LEFT AND RIGHT

If we look again at the patterning of the layout, we can find two more triads, facing left and right, with the cards in the vertical center line partaking of both. These triads are closely associated with the idea of time and also show the unified sense of time governing the whole reading. This center line is the now, the temporal aspect of our lives running from past to present to future. From the standpoint of now, we can look both backward as we remember and forward as we project into the future. But the top and bottom cards of the reading, where these two triads conjoin, also indicate that there are factors that stand beyond the normal flow of chronological time. Usually, in a reading the question or situation does not cover a very long period of time—a few years at most— so we don't have to dig too deep to understand how two Tarot symbols may represent the essence of this entire time span. For instance, if the Lover sits at the top of the reading and the Devil at the bottom, then it is clear that for the entire time span of this reading the querent has been almost literally stuck on the horns of a dilemma. And if the rest of the spread indicates that this is indeed a difficult situation, then the Tarot reader might look for ways in which this tension can be released: how to act so that the arrow is finally fired and the decision made, and how to dismiss the Devil from his over-exalted perch in the person's psyche, where he perhaps represents domination by guilt or past obligations.

Each triad also contains transitional cards (to be considered again shortly) showing how there is movement from one phase to another. As with the above and below triads, it can be helpful to allow our gaze to rest on these left and right triads when looking at the overall layout in a reading. The notion of gazing into the Fool's mirror as part of the practice of divination will be discussed a little later in this chapter.

Within the span of the two sets of triads—above and below, left and right—we can pinpoint their components more closely. Although we have covered this already to some extent, it is worth recapping and adding a little more to the definitions.

PAST, PRESENT, AND FUTURE

The reading is divided into left-, center, and right-hand columns, representing past, present, and future. Again, it's important to keep to this. There could be other ways of interpreting this spatial relationship that are *not* relevant here. For instance, there is no implication in the Fool's Mirror layout that left is negative, passive, or bad, with right as its opposite. Here the definition is the division of time.

THE TOP AND BOTTOM CARDS (18 AND 19)

The top and bottom cards are often very important in the reading. We've already looked at their function both in the preliminary exercises in this chapter and as unifiers in terms of chronological time, but it may be helpful to expand their significance. In terms of the above and below triangles, the topmost card (18) represents the apex, the driving force or expression of the situation "out there." The bottommost card (19) summarizes the internal motivation of the individual in question at present, or the hidden force underpinning a situation. The interplay of the two can also be considered. For instance, if a person has asked about his current employment and the top card (18) is the Wheel of Fortune and the bottom card (19) is the Chariot, it may be appropriate to say (taking other cards and positions into account): "You are at heart very ambitious, but in your current work you're subject to too many changes outside your control to achieve your aims."

Then, as we have just seen, these two cards act as the essence of the moment in time in which the question is asked; they carry the actions of the past and the potency of the future within them. Although they are placed on the central column of the reading, they reign over the other two triads, the left- and right-hand sides of the second double diamond, pointing backward and forward in time. They are the ultimate factors in the now of the reading.

So in one sense these two cards, at the peak and depth of the reading, are the governors of the situation, denoting the wholeness and integrity of the reading. They are always worthy of intense scrutiny.

THE FOUR TRANSITIONAL CARDS (14–17)

The four transitional cards fill in the space between the core cards of the three time phases and the culminating cards at the top and bottom. They are nos. 14, 15, 16, and 17. In the key points, I called them "the carriers of change." They are the stepping-stones from past to present, present to future. In my experience, they have a different kind of shading from the other cards. They seem to point to more ephemeral states of being, or changing forces within the situation. They may indicate the reason why things have moved on, or will move on, including an unexpected factor that arose or a change of heart. My own take on these is to give them due consideration, and then to decide within the context of the reading whether they have particular importance or not. They may help you to understand the flow of the reading, but they do not always need close analysis when you give the interpretation. Our aim should be to include every card within the overall interpretation, but it isn't always necessary to discuss every card individually or to the same extent. Having said that, these four cards do have a kind of magical quality, but they may also be elusive, like the stuff of dreams. And, as such, they play their part. Look to them to give you a sense of flow.

THE CENTER LINE: THE DUOS (2–7)

The six cards along the central line (nos. 2, 3, 4, 5, 6, and 7) are often the most intriguing, as the pairings spark off against one another. Here we may find alliances, conflicts, and striking combinations of energies. What might the Empress be doing with Justice, for instance? Is a woman who abuses her power about to get her just deserts? Or will a woman who has perhaps been rather weak now find her inner strength and fight for justice? These are just two of the ways in which a pairing can generate meaning, and you'll need to judge it on the overall spread of the cards and the question being asked. This is the place where it all happens, where one's inner world and external forces collide. Or harmonize. Or form an uneasy alliance. If it helps, you can attribute the left-hand card to the internal side of the situation and the right-hand card to the external situation. This can be a useful aid to reading the pair as a duo.

TWO SETS OF THREE: THE OUTER (8, 10, AND 12) AND INNER (9, 11, AND 13) LEVELS

The cards in positions 8, 10, and 12 represent the most immediately discernible effects on the outer level, and those in 9, 11, and 13 those on the inner level; we have already practiced these, but it is worth emphasizing their importance here. They are solid, dependable cards in a reading and tend to give a clear indication of what is actually happening both "out there" and "inside." They are useful reference points if one is struggling to make sense of the duo sets of cards along the center line.

To take a couple of examples—always depending upon the subject of the question, of course—if in the "now" section of the reading no. 10 in its position above the center line is filled by the Tower, then the querent is almost certainly suffering some kind of loss. For instance, their business is losing money, even if they protest that everything is fine. If no. 11, below the line, is the Sun, then the person is definitely in a happy phase and has good sources of energy. My recommendation for these positions is not to be too subtle. Read it like it is.

THE SIGNIFICATOR

The sole card that starts the reading is the last to be considered here within the main body of the layout. This is because it has less geometrical or symbolic significance, and we have already worked with its intrinsic meaning. However, everything relates back to it. In the Fool's Mirror spread, it is always drawn from the pack unseen after shuffling, never chosen deliberately to represent the question or querent, as with some Tarot layouts. It is therefore a "divined" card, drawn as the supreme indicator that determines the nature and scope of the question.

THE THREE SECRET CARDS

The three cards that are left facedown add a touch of mystery to the reading. They represent the reason why the question was asked, or the elements that are lacking in a particular situation. If nothing were missing, would anything change? If we weren't driven by what we lack, we might not act. Of course, anyone who is experienced with the Tarot can work out quite quickly which three cards are not present in the open spread of cards. But most querents won't do that, and I recommend that as reader of the cards you also leave aside any mental calculations of what they might be, at least in the early stages of the reading. Their proper impact should come at the end, when they are turned faceup and interpreted, as will be described in the section about the sequence of the reading. It's the moment when the diviner can say, "This is what's lacking at present—this is what you really want" and see the querent's face light up in joy. Sometimes I've noticed that this is when the tension dissolves on a person's face, because it's the point in the reading when he or she feels truly understood.

This moment of adjustment, of resolution, is well placed right at the end of the session, because the seeking quality that infuses the main part of the reading is needed to tease out the questions and the truth of the situation. The matter is not yet laid to rest. At the end, the missing pieces of the jigsaw puzzle are offered, but only after any difficulties or dilemmas have been considered. The main part of the reading will hopefully sharpen the querent's resolve to make decisions and to face up to the prevailing circumstances. Then this last piece of understanding can bring a sense of completion and confidence in one's worth.

As touched on in the exercises for card positions, it is possible to read the three cards separately or together. Each one may represent a different aspect of life that is in abeyance at the moment, or they may make more sense as a combined trio. Sometimes it may be possible to include both aspects in the interpretation; but if in doubt, treat each card separately and quite simply.

PREPARING FOR THE READING

This now covers the theory of the layout. But a Tarot reading—as I discover anew, writing this book—is an onion with many layers. Even after many years of experience, questions and challenges still arise, especially with a fully inclusive layout such as this one. So along with clarifying the sequence of giving a reading, I also offer some guidance as to how to go about it, as distilled from the teachings passed down to me and my own long-term practice of reading the cards.

WHOM TO READ FOR

The first decision you will have to make is whether to accept a request to give a reading. Here's an early warning list of those people with whom one should proceed cautiously:

* People close to you—especially partners, parents, and children
* Someone who is in an agitated state
* Someone who is very demanding in their request
* Someone who wants to put the system to the test
* Yourself

If your life is entwined with someone, you may be too anxious on their behalf, or have too fixed a view of who they are and what they should do. The decision is yours, but I recommend thinking through the consequences first. Consider what effect the reading might have on the person, if it strikes home with them—and also if it doesn't. Would this shift the balance in your relationship, perhaps adversely?

Out of this emerges a golden guideline:

Try to read the cards for someone as though you really don't know them. Be open to the possibilities in the cards even if you do back these up with a little sneaky knowledge of that person. Let the cards do the talking—not your inbuilt ideas.

I have proved the wisdom of this to myself many times in divination practice, usually through being tempted to ignore this advice!

Of course, people may often want a reading when they are going through a crisis or have a particular worry. But the calmer they can be at the time of the reading, the better. For one thing, they may simply not listen properly to what you tell them. We've all been to the doctor and forgotten most of what we were told because we were preoccupied with our worries. Make your own judgment on this; if you feel someone is too upset to proceed, you can either try to calm the person with a short preamble—a light-hearted chat, some music, or a quick cup of coffee can often set the balance right—or ask them to come back later. Tarot is not a "rescue remedy," and it shouldn't be treated as an emergency prop.

You always have the right to refuse to do a reading. If someone puts undue pressure on you and you feel uneasy, my advice is to find a pleasant way to decline. It may be a sign that their expectations are too high or they have an unwarranted sense of entitlement. Divination is not a push-button activity. It can be difficult turning people away, but it is probably easier to do that at the outset than further along the line. Pressure to accept the request may mean that there will be pressure on you during the reading to deliver in the way the other person expects. You need to be free to work in your own way, with mental space to contemplate what the cards are communicating.

If you do refuse, try to make it sound as though it's not personal and you aren't rejecting the individual concerned. To avoid any awkwardness, it may be better to respond initially to requests in a way that leaves matters open. For example, by saying, "You'd like a Tarot reading? Can you say a little more, so that I can figure out if I can help you, and if this is the best moment for it?" If you are not sure about someone but don't want to dismiss their request out of hand, you can always ask them to contact you later on and reassess the situation then. One of the old principles of esoteric training was that a person should ask three times before being admitted, and in fact this is not a bad way to work. Even though you might admire a person's tenacity, if you still feel at the third time of asking that it is not appropriate to read the cards for them, then be kind but firm, and deter them once and for all.

The "test" is a perennial problem for astrologers, dowsers, card readers, rune casters, and diviners of sundry kinds. The person who treats the reading as some kind of test, or proof, is approaching with a closed mind and will accept only certain kinds of results. Again, if you feel backed into a corner, you may prefer to refuse. An effective divination reading depends on both minds being open to a truth emerging. Some people like to rise to the challenge, and if you're one of them, fair enough. But beware: the danger to the Tarot reader, as I see it, is that treating the reading as some kind of a contest can cloud one's own motivations, and the end result may upset one or both parties.

A final note on this topic: the "tester" is not the same as the "innocent fool" who asks for a reading. Sometimes people come with no preconceptions, or even any particular expectation that a Tarot reading will work, but they are prepared to give it a go. Such readings can produce stunning results for this "innocent fool." There are no prejudices and no great desires—excellent conditions for a reading.

Tarot is an intuitive, fluid medium of divination. In my view, it is not suitable for self-analysis or prediction for oneself. Not everyone would agree with this. But it's easy for fears and hopes to grow out of proportion in the process of doing the reading, along with mistaken ideas about what can happen. A Tarot reader needs a degree of initial detachment, which is almost impossible to have in this case. My advice is to ask someone else to do a reading for you. Having said that, I think it's fine to use the cards to inquire about an outside situation you're interested in, or perhaps even about another person who is not present, as long as you're happy that this is appropriate. It's when the main focus is on one's own psyche that the distorting mirrors can come into play. We try to keep the reflection in the Fool's mirror as clear as possible.

THE SEQUENCE OF THE FOOL'S MIRROR READING

The sequence here is relatively straightforward and similar to that recommended by many other Tarot readers. You may find ways in which you wish to vary it in practice.

The person asking the question will be referred to as the querent. If you are both querent and reader, then it's simple enough to merge the steps. Additional advice supplementing the main aspects of the procedure is in italics.

Formulating the Question

The reader invites the querent to choose either a specific question or a general reading of their current situation. If the querent needs help in defining a question or determining its suitability for the reading, this should be discussed before the shuffle. Sometimes the querent prefers to remain silent about the reading's exact nature at the beginning, in which case the reader will try to determine it through the reading itself. However, this can make matters harder, and you can develop a personal strategy on this. You may decide that you will proceed with a reading only if the querent is prepared to speak the question aloud at the start, and make that a condition of offering to read, or you might be willing to take on the challenge of discovering the question once the cards are set out.

Instructions for the Layout

The querent shuffles the cards thoroughly until he or she feels that they are ready and then places them face-down on the table. (Watch out for someone who goes into a shuffling trance! Usually, people bring it to a rest themselves, but occasionally it's necessary to ask them to stop.)

The querent cuts the deck in two with his or her non-dominant hand (sometimes called the hand of the unconscious) and then places the bottom half on top of the other half of the deck. Then he or she carries out the cut-and-replace sequence twice more. Some people find this procedure confusing. You could have a spare set of cards handy to demonstrate if so.

The reader takes the pack and fans out the cards, with the backs of the cards facing the querent. The reader then asks the querent to pick one card out of the pack.

The reader takes this card and places it faceup on what will be the left-hand side of the layout. This is the significator of the reading, no. 1 on the diagram.

The Fool's Mirror reading takes up a lot of space. Make sure you have plenty to begin with; you need to be able to continue uninterrupted once you've started, as it would disturb the atmosphere to move the cards once you are laying out the spread.

The reader continues by laying down the cards faceup in the order of the reading until the first row is complete—cards 1–7 inclusive. Then he or she must check if the Fool is present.

Finding the Fool

If the Fool is the significator, that is fine. This means that the querent is receptive to the way the reading will reveal itself. It is a sign of true openness and willingness to know.

If the Fool is hidden in the remaining three cards that lie facedown, that is also fine. It could refer to a loss of innocence or a lack of spontaneity in the current situation.

If the Fool appears in the central row of the reading (nos. 2–7), it invalidates the reading in this method of Tarot divination. It means that either the reader or the querent has some bias or preconception or does not really want to know what the cards say. When this happens, the reader invites both parties to reflect quietly on the situation for a couple of minutes. Then the reader can ask the querent if he or she would like to try again—that's if the reader has discovered no fundamental misgivings about continuing. If both wish to continue, the reader puts all the cards back into the pack and invites the querent to shuffle and go through the process again.

If this happens three times (which is rare), the reading is canceled for the moment. It could be helpful for the reader and the querent to discuss why they think this has happened. If neither of them knows, one way to end the session on a positive note is to say that perhaps there are imminent changes about to take place, and it's better to wait awhile and see what happens first. I suggest that a minimum of three days should pass before another attempt is made. The reader should in no way bind the querent to try again. Tarot readings aren't for everyone.

Assuming the Fool is in an acceptable position, the reader completes the layout and lays the three final cards facedown to one side of the reading, or even places them elsewhere.

Sometimes the querent asks what the facedown cards are. It's not a bad idea to allow a little sense of mystery to develop and say that they should remain hidden or secret until the end.

Now the cards are ready to be interpreted.

A SAMPLE READING

When I first began working with the Fool's Mirror layout, I felt daunted by the fact that I was going to have to include all of the cards in the divination, even the three that were kept to one side. It would also mean that I couldn't rely on the kind of obvious signposting that comes with the layouts where only certain cards are dealt from the pack, as the important elements of the question are then automatically defined by the cards that are drawn. I had to admit too that I felt I would miss the sense of excitement as the cards are laid out, wondering which ones will be revealed this time.

The need to cover every card in a Tarot reading was indeed a challenge. Would I be swimming helplessly, with no firm ground to rest my feet on? I soon learned, however, that although it could be a demanding process, it was one that I could cope with. I discovered that there are natural contours and definitions within the all-card layout: Some Tarot Trumps scarcely need individual interpretation, as they meld into a combined meaning with others. Others stand out within the reading and need more emphasis in their interpretation. Overall, the Fool's Mirror layout is a kind of mandala, a mirror reflecting the state of play containing all the elements and creating a whole picture. Within that picture are light and shade, some strongly defined shapes, and other more subtle alignments. Even the "missing" cards, in temporary eclipse, are a part of this.[1]

One of the best ways to start reading the Fool's Mirror layout is to have someone read the cards for you this way. I was lucky; it's how I came across the layout and experienced it in the first instance. My Tarot teacher, Glyn, both interpreted it for me and taught it to me. The chances are that this will be your first encounter with the layout, though, and I can only do my best here to lead you into it via the book and via encouraging you to practice. But if you wish to pass it on to others in due course, I do recommend that you offer a reading as part of the instruction. This way, although not every detail of the card positions may be clarified immediately, the layout imprints itself in the psyche, and a real connection with the cards can be established.

A GUINEA PIG READING

At this point, I recommend trying out a sample reading. In my view, doing a complete dummy reading based on an imaginary querent and/or question runs counter to the spirit of divination (a point I will explore more fully in the next chapter). But it is possible to do a step-by-step reading for a friendly person who doesn't mind being a guinea pig. And, if you have no guinea pig handy, you could try a speculative reading for a question that you pose yourself, as explained below.

If you invite someone to take part in a practice reading, make it clear that you are in the early stages of working with this layout and that you will probably be working rather slowly and methodically. Say that you might need to ask questions as you go; in this instance it's likely that you will want confirmation as to whether the interpretation is going along the right lines, in terms of the situation that the querent has asked about.

I strongly suggest that you make this reading one based on the querent's general situation, rather than to answer a specific question. It might sound as though a defined question would be easier—and it probably is with the less detailed layouts that we've already worked with—but for the Fool's Mirror layout, it is actually more appropriate and easier to use it as a reflection of the person's state. You are not then compelled to give an "answer," either, which the querent might anticipate from posing a clearly defined question.

Do not expect too much of yourself at this point. By all means, engage fully, but regard it as "work in progress" and tell your subject the same. It can still be of value for both of you. Many people who ask for readings will be quite happy with whatever you can give them on this occasion, even if it's just a few pointers and tips, rather than a seamlessly presented interpretation. They are likely to enjoy the experience and take something away from it.

In fact, although your initial process to the reading may seem rather disjointed, you may well find that once you've completed the step-by-step analysis, you can move into a different phase and explore more intuitively how it all fits together. But this may not happen straightaway, and you might prefer to do a short series of guinea pig readings before you attempt to do a fully integrated interpretation.

Before we move on to questions about Tarot practice in general, there are a couple more issues that I raise for consideration, which may help to light the way into this Fool's Mirror mode of reading.

THE SPREAD

All twenty-two Tarot Trumps are used in this layout, including the three hidden cards. It will therefore come as no surprise when any particular card shows its face in the reading. In other words, no sharp intake of breath should occur if Death or the Devil appears. They will inevitably be somewhere in the mix, and they must be accommodated in the reading. As we have seen, the initial D here does not equate doom or demons, and these two cards can often suggest constructive forces, or at least a necessary struggle within the course of affairs. In terms of Death, for instance, one form is always giving way to another, and so Death in that sense is always present. A good guideline for interpreting the Death card within this layout is to ask: what is currently dying away and being replaced by something new?

The twenty-two archetypes here represent a complete mirror of the human psyche or a situation. All are at work in shaping that picture, and all must be considered. The Fool's Mirror layout thus safeguards Tarot readers from making too much of the appearance of the less "fortunate" cards and seeing them too readily as harbingers of a gloomy fate. The fact that all the cards are included puts a useful brake on interpreting the less attractive ones in their darkest sense.

GAZING INTO THE FOOL'S MIRROR

How can we start to see this kind of reading as a whole? What method or technique—if any—can help to develop this process? It is all very well to say that when you take on this layout of the Fool's Mirror you can begin to allow intuition and inner knowledge to come through. But how can we trigger this?

First of all, in terms of the way the basic reading takes place, it's important to use the navigational aids—the positions of the cards—to give useful bearings on the reading and to shape the interpretation in terms of the how, where, and when of the situation. That nuts-and-bolts aspect of divination should not be bypassed with this reading; it is not an act of pure psychism, but one where we use all our faculties and acquired knowledge to give the gist of the interpretation. But the real subtlety, the power and unique life of the reading, ultimately depends on a kind of "seeing." The next stage, therefore, after analyzing the card positions is to look at the cards as a complete picture; we can then begin to see the dynamics much better: the contours, the emphases, the alliances, and struggles within that spread.

The Art of Gazing

Taking this a step further, we can aspire to move into a different realm of perception. At this point, we not only see the reading as a complete entity but can also let it speak to us. This can be described as a process of "gazing." It is not a trance, but it does mean allowing ourselves to let go of worded interpretations and move into a more indefinite, expansive state as we let go of the normal analytical process and become receptive to the picture that the Tarot Triumphs present. From this may come a general sense of the essential truth of the reading, or a flash or two of inspiration as to what certain elements of it mean. Or maybe nothing much seems to happen, just a change of awareness. But even out of this "nothingness" something may emerge, forming itself into a new confidence when we speak about the reading to the querent. Perhaps we may find ourselves saying things that we didn't know we knew beforehand.

This is not mediumship, as it requires remaining conscious of ourselves and the world around us. It is more akin to a form of contemplation. Also, in the Fool's Mirror approach it is imperative that the Tarot reader take full responsibility for his or her words and never approach the reading as a kind of mediumistic activity, seeing it as a vehicle to encourage another voice or spirit to speak. What we are trying to do is align ourselves with a greater source of knowledge, which comes from allowing our own consciousness to open up while putting words and preformed ideas to one side. But then, our task is to put our own words upon what we perceive.

How can we generate this "gazing" in a reading? You will need to experiment a little to find out what works best for you. I have a naturally analytical mind that pounces on points of interest, so the best approach for me personally, and probably for most people, is to study the reading in its component parts first. Then I allow myself to sink back into a more restful state for a few minutes, gazing at the entire layout and letting the sense of it develop. I aim to allow it to come into my consciousness as a whole, as an integrated pattern. This means that reading the Fool's Mirror layout does take longer than interpreting a simpler layout with selected cards, such as the basic Celtic Cross formation. I usually warn the querent that I may be silent for a while, and that this is nothing for them to be anxious about. But you may find that you prefer to gaze at the spread soon after it is laid out and then go into a more specific interpretation afterward.

When you reach this point, make sure that you are well rooted in your own physical position; it can be helpful to bring back the attention to the body and sense it as a whole for a few moments. Then turn your attention back to the Tarot Triumphs and allow your gaze to encompass the whole layout. Imagine that you are the Fool, in the very best sense of divine openness, and that the Tarot symbols are reflected in your mirror that you hold to witness the sacred workings of creation. Let the gaze rest there, keeping it wide, wider than the actual physical dimensions of the layout, and retain this sense of expansiveness lightly, so that it does not narrow down again.

As I've already implied, this is a process in its own right, akin to the nature of spiritual contemplation. It may not deliver an instant reading of the cards, but once the general gazing has taken place, you may find that you can ask the cards if you have questions, and listen for the answers. It can be particularly helpful, for instance, if you have already studied most of the individual cards and their positions but are left with some questions about them that puzzle you. By all means, pose the questions; but let the response come to you, or not, as the case may be. Never force it. If an answer doesn't come at once, it may come a little later.

COMMON MIND

I have suggested that this switch into another state of awareness is the stage at which intuition may come into play. But what does this mean? It means reaching into a different kind of knowledge, one not usually prevalent in our usual mode of being. The type of consciousness involved may not be hugely different from our normal state, but it is one where the usual train of associations and so-called reason are more subdued and a state of receptiveness arises. Some would say that this taps into our unconscious. Others, myself included, suggest that this is in fact a greater form of consciousness, of a more far-reaching and inclusive kind. One of the most enlightening quotations that I have found about this state comes from the ancient Hermetic writings dating from the earliest centuries CE. Here *gnosis* equates with "knowledge"; it is our birthright, but only for those who wish to claim it.

It was [God's] will . . . that mind should be placed in the midst as a prize that human souls may win . . . He filled a great basin with mind and sent it down to earth; and he appointed a herald, and bade him make a proclamation to the hearts of men: "Hearken, each human heart; dip yourself in this basin, if you can, recognizing for what purpose you have been made, and believing that you shall ascend to Him who sent the basin down." Now those who gave heed to the proclamation, and dipped themselves in the bath of mind, these men got a share of gnosis; they received mind and so became complete men.[2]

The "basin of mind," a wonderfully evocative image, could also be called "common mind," or the "mind of mankind." The gazing process I've just described can be a way of dipping into this common mind, which in itself is a part of consciousness in its widest sense.

Biologists are beginning to play with the idea of species mind, and I believe it will become increasingly important in our understanding of the universe in the next hundred years or so.[3] If we begin to admit the concept of a "permeable" individuality and to accept that we are connected to a wider sphere of consciousness, then this also helps us understand how we can receive knowledge and intimations from a source that is definitely not personal, in the normal sense. Telepathy becomes part of the normal range of possible human abilities, instead of being dismissed as something odd, supernatural, or downright impossible. This is nothing new; many tribespeople have never forgotten it, children frequently display it, and some of us are naturally inclined that way, despite the efforts of a "modern" viewpoint to promote only what can be proven scientifically. And in the context here, it could be a useful way of understanding how a Tarot reading works and how we might try to use such a faculty.

KNOWLEDGE AS THE REWARD OF TAROT

This leads us to the understanding that reading the cards can be a way of expanding individual consciousness and entering a greater sphere of knowledge. Opening up our inner senses can bring us much closer to that source of knowledge, knowledge that can inform us in a way ordinary analysis struggles to achieve. It is why, I believe, reading the Tarot can be so fulfilling in its own right. The experience is less about the ego I and more about the discovery of a wider domain of knowledge. It is accompanied by letting go of more personal thoughts and concerns, and sensing a fusion of one's own mind with something that is greater.

Such a reading doesn't happen all the time. But if you put in the time to learn the symbolism, master the technique, and use this inclusive layout, there is a good chance that it may occur. We do need the symbols and the structure to give the foundation for the reading; it wouldn't happen without them. The reward of Tarot reading is not just about pride in "getting it right," or even helping someone in a fix, good as those outcomes may be. Entering a state of knowledge engenders a feeling of wonder and of being fully alive. It springs the prison doors of our usual petty worries and indulgences. This goes for both the Tarot reader and the person asking the question.

The answers may not come in the form expected, but that person can be left with a sense of a wisdom that brings far-sighted reassurance to the turbulence of life. The Tarot reader is not the "owner" of that wisdom, but they can help to manifest it through their receptivity to what the cards declare.

In summary, that feeling of wonder indicates both the challenge and the joy of working with this particular layout. It offers the chance to read the situation as a whole and connect with a living picture rather than a series of disjointed meanings, or a string of set attributions. The Fool's Mirror grants a unified vision of how events and inner states of mind interact, and how past, present, and future, although separate in one way, are at their root conjoined. It can certainly require effort to understand and communicate that, but our standpoint as witnesses to the bigger picture is a privileged one.

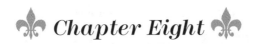

Chapter Eight

MANAGING THE READING

Reading the Tarot is a magical act. This is not the magic of popular imagination, full of exotic props and incantations, but a quieter way to generate truth-telling through bringing our hearts and minds into alignment with the cards and with the spirit of the Tarot tradition. So the ways in which we set the scene, greet the person who has come for a reading, and stage the sequence of actions are all part and parcel of what can be called the ritual of divination practice.

We aim to set up conditions in which a higher under-standing can be present, generated by the act of asking the question with good intentions and laying out the cards in an appropriate manner. This can help to open up a sacred space in which the meaning of the cards can shine forth. The ritual of the reading may therefore take us across the threshold from the ordinary world into one of heightened significance, where symbols act as the lan-guage of revelation and a skillful reader and a receptive subject can divine their meaning. The manner in which we conduct the reading and conclude it is also a part of this practice, rounding off the process so that we can make a smooth transition back into our normal activities and state of mind.

All of this is magical, in the sense that it can generate a transformative, illuminating experience, something perhaps beyond what we could achieve by ordinary investigation and discussion. In other words, developing some simple ritual for the process of Tarot divination is highly recommended even in the most casual of circumstances. Both diviner and querent need a prompt to move into this arena of discovery even for the shortest or simplest of readings.

SETTING THE SCENE

In the Fool's Mirror method of divination, I was taught that you can usually make do with the surroundings you find yourself in, and you can make the space work in a very simple way, provided you follow some basic principles of setting it up. You can adapt these according to your circumstances and your personal taste. You may indeed choose to have mysterious silver-shot curtains, rose-colored lighting, crystals on the table, and a room full of strange and wonderful objects if you wish, but it's not essential. It may even prove cumbersome; too much paraphernalia can clutter the mind and even cloud the intention of the divination. As with other types of ritual, if we try to understand the principles involved in their most essential form, then we can have more choices as to how we implement them and more flexibility in adapting to different circumstances and settings if need be.

WORKING SPACE

So, what is essential for a full Tarot reading? A good working space is the priority. Aim to do the following:

1. Find a space that is quiet, one where you won't be interrupted or overlooked. This allows the reader to concentrate and the querent to relax.

2. If you have time beforehand, tidy or order the space so that you feel purposeful and ready to work, and arrange it so as to be comfortable for your guest.

3. Designate a sizeable table or broad area on which to lay out the cards—the floor can be fine if you don't mind sitting at ground level.

4. Request that all cell phones be turned off when you and the querent are ready to start. It is important that both of you are willing to put aside your normal props and enter the arena of divination.

If you cannot give the reading in a private place, then distil the main requirements down to what you can manage in the situation—as quiet a corner as possible, one where you won't be overlooked and where you both stow away personal items that are irrelevant to the reading.

RITUALS FOR PROTECTION

You may wish to do a simple ritual to bless and protect the space you are working in, especially if you are concerned that it is not as secure and bounded as you might like. For instance, maybe there is a risk of someone interrupting, or of distracting activities nearby, or noise just outside. Or perhaps you sense that the other person is upset or very restless.

The following is a protection ritual that I was taught many years ago and have found to be very effective:

Once you and the querent are settled in your places, imagine four very tall winged blue figures, one standing in each corner of the room. Their wings are folded when you first visualize the figures, but once they are in position allow them to spread their wings so that the tip of each wing touches the tip of the next wing of the figure that stands in the adjacent corner. The wings thus meet along the sides of the room and the space is enclosed by them. Trust that their presence will remain throughout the session; you do not need to pay attention to them while the reading is going on.

At the end of the session, before anyone leaves the room, bring the figures to mind again, say a silent thank you to them for their protection, and bid them depart. If you have to go out at any point during the reading, this should be fine; just call their presence back to mind as you exit and enter again. This is a gentle protection, not a complete barring of the doors. This visualization should be kept private, and you do not need to tell the other person what you are doing; just close your eyes for a few seconds. If necessary, explain that you are taking a quiet moment to prepare.

If you prefer something simpler, or in accordance with your particular faith, you could recite a prayer either aloud before the other person enters or silently when you are both seated. This is well within traditional divinatory and healing practices; in Russian folk tradition, country people would say a prayer to the Mother of God before they picked herbs for medicinal purposes.[1] Alternatively, you could devise a brief request such as, "May this reading be truthful and bring benefit to the person seeking it." It can be offered to the spirit and lineage of the Tarot, if you like, rather than as a more prayerful utterance.

Again, you do not have to share your ritual or prayer with the other person. Tarot reading is a cooperative but not necessarily democratic process. Setting up the space is the diviner's task, to be done with goodwill as he or she sees fit, and the process need not be explained to the querent. The querent is, or should be, largely in receptive mode, as someone who comes with a genuine question and is open to understanding what the cards might reveal. The job at hand for the Tarot practitioner is therefore to set up the best conditions for this reading.

Even if you don't choose an overtly ritual practice, be aware of the need to collect yourself and to quieten heart and mind; you might find you can do this even while chatting in a leisurely way to the person who is asking for the reading. You can also find ways of introducing a little space for reflection into the reading, something that can help the querent too. For instance, when you're ready to start, hold the pack of cards in your hand and suggest that you both close your eyes and stay silent for a few moments. Ask the querent to focus on the question or situation they are planning to inquire about. Then, take the lead in ending the silence and move on decisively. This sets the tone and gives confidence through establishing a clear sequence and an unruffled presence.

THE SACRED MOMENT OF THE READING

Divination is linked to time. We ask a question at a particular moment in time, and the answer that comes emerges from that moment. Even if the question has been mulled over for a long time, the act of asking it, of shuffling and laying out the cards, produces what is in effect a unique situation. The specific way the cards fall out for a Tarot reading is born out of this moment of asking the question. The chemistry between reader and querent is also in a particular balance at this time, and the way the interpretation is spoken and received is bound up with this relationship. In other words, a Tarot reading will never be exactly the same twice.

Certain things follow from this: chiefly, that a Tarot spread *must* be read at the time it's laid out. Do not lay it out and come back to it later. Do not revisit a reading that you did earlier. We read the cards as best we can according to the conditions of that moment and need to accept that we cannot perfect this at a later stage. Many is the time that I have thought of something afterward that I wished I had said to the person for whom I gave the reading, but I have learnt to be firm with myself. If I didn't think of it at the time, then it has no place in the reading now. If I speak of it later it counts as unsolicited advice, and that is not part of the Tarot reader's remit.

The importance of the relationship between diviner, querent, cards, and the moment of time is also why I don't offer full dummy readings for the Fool's Mirror layout. I don't believe it's possible to create an authentic reading in a vacuum by laying out the cards as if for a real question or a real person. That undermines the principle of true divination practice, which is never a mechanical affair, but always dependent upon the grace of the moment. I have shown how we can take limited combinations of cards for practice runs, but to my mind it is inappropriate to pretend that a whole divination layout is "real." This blurs the boundaries and produces an uneasy "phantom" reading. At best, to lay out a full Fool's Mirror spread for a fake question will produce a flat, weary kind of reading that doesn't have the spark and truth of a genuine one.

ENDING THE READING

Clear away the reading as soon as you feel the discussion has come to the end of its useful run. You may choose to sit for a few minutes with the querent after you've reached the end of your interpretation and chat in a lighter way about what's been discovered, but don't let this run on too long. Close the reading by putting away the cards before the energy runs out. I also like to shuffle the cards loosely before I do this so that the reading is dispelled. If necessary, change your seating positions or go to another room so that you remove yourselves physically from the divination situation. If you've used the winged beings protection ritual, you can take a moment to mentally dissolve the image.

Try not to worry about the reading later, and wonder whether you said "the right thing." We've all done that, but not every reading blossoms; sometimes the person asking the question resists the process, and that can make it harder for the reader. Later on, you may learn more about the particular situation or events involved and will realize that it wasn't your fault that the reading didn't go as well as you'd hoped. We all want to prove ourselves as accomplished Tarot readers, but the reality is that we are at the mercy of the moment, and it won't always work out that way.

Another word of advice on this: resist the temptation to pick up with the querent later and gain reassurance from them that the reading was fine. Letting go of the session is important; otherwise the waters may be muddied. Only in rare cases is it a good idea to make further inquiries after the reading: for instance, if the person suffered some kind of emotional upheaval during the reading. There could be a case then for offering further support through talking about what happened, although if you are not a qualified therapist I strongly recommend that you keep the boundaries clear on that score. Usually the querent will absorb the reading in their own way and take from it what they need without any further intervention. Your gift to the person is to let them take the reading away and relinquish any claims of ownership yourself.

CLOSING RITUAL

Occasionally, you may find it hard to dispel the atmosphere left by the reading. Perhaps you sense a lingering presence or emotional imbalance that disturbs the equilibrium of the room. If so, then you may need to banish this in order to restore normality. This is not necessarily anything unearthly; a visitor who is depressed, angry, or fearful, for instance, can leave traces of their feelings behind in the room, like a lingering scent. It's also possible that the divination session could leave a highly charged atmosphere, something that was very productive in terms of the reading but not suitable to sustain beyond that.

In either case, if the normal finishing-off of the practice doesn't lay the energies to rest, there is a simple remedy for clearing the space. When you have the room to yourself, find a couple of small stones that make a distinct sound when you hit them against one other. Move around the space, briskly clacking the stones here and there, in the corners, in the center, around the edges. Open the door, perhaps open a window, and let the air come through. That will usually do the trick.

ETHICS AND OUTLOOK OF THE READING

Here are some further ethical, practical, and philosophical considerations for you to reflect on. They are not set in stone, but they should help you to develop your Tarot practice in a mature and individual way.

Discretion

Keep anything you learn about the other person in confidence. Don't be tempted to mention what went on even to your partner, or to capitalize on any secrets you may have learnt. If in a very rare case you learn about criminal activity, or something that vitally affects another person within your circle—for example, an ongoing affair or a serious illness concealed from a spouse—you will have to reconsider this principle and make a decision on what is best. It's beyond my remit to advise you in this case, but I suggest that you take action only if it is absolutely necessary to do so.

I prefer to "forget" my readings after I've finished. I do not want to be in any way burdened with someone else's business, nor do I want to gather any sense of power that might accrue from giving an effective reading. That too would be a burden. Like most readers, I probably feel delighted when a reading has apparently gone well, and I can't deny that it gives me a boost. But overall, it's the sense of entering that place of knowledge that brings me the greatest sense of fulfillment.

Keeping Notes

If you plan to keep a record of your readings, as for a casebook, it is probably best to mention this to the querent beforehand, reassuring them that you will keep all stories anonymous. If the querent is adamant that no notes should be kept at all, then this view should be respected. If you do make a record, I recommend putting it away and not looking at it for several months so that you can mentally step away from the divination. By the time you look at the notes again, there will be a degree of detachment from the reading.

A practical hint: it may be simpler and less intrusive to take a quick photo of the layout rather than writing down all the card positions of a reading. Try not to write notes at the time of the interpretation; it can be off-putting for both parties, and you'll remember enough to jot them down afterward.

The High Place

One of my favorite alchemical engravings depicts a mountaintop where a winged guide leads the seeker up to a high place and shows him the view, the terrain that lies around the mountain.[2] I find this a beautiful and very pertinent image for the process of giving a divination reading, and I like to bring it to mind frequently in this context. The reader's role, as I see it, is to try to act as this kind of guide, someone who can show the querent the view from that high place. This is where a new perspective can be gained, and new hope generated by seeing the landscape as a whole.

Both reader and querent have to make the effort to scale the mountain. The reader does not own that view, nor is it the job of the reader to lead the querent through that terrain. The aim is to take them up the mountain to the "high place," reveal what can be seen from there, and guide them safely down again. If we can do all this, it's a job well done. What the seeker makes of that view is up to him; what path he then takes through the terrain is his choice.

Empathy and Responsibility

However clear the view from the top of the mountain, or in the layout of the Tarot cards, we as readers still need to take great care how we deliver our findings. It can be appropriate to show sympathy if someone is distressed, but it is important too to keep steering the reading with clarity. A Tarot reader swamped by emotion will ruin the whole process and may leave the querent without any firm ground to stand on. While a degree of empathy is welcome in a reading, too much can be disastrous.

If the cards seem to offer a harsh outlook, then you might wish to soften the way in which you deliver this interpretation without speaking outright lies. Often the best way to approach this is to convey that although the situation may be difficult, there is a positive side to it. The Fool's Mirror layout is on our side in this respect because every card is present, so no particular card can be indicative of a negative outcome simply by appearing in the reading. By training ourselves to see all the different aspects of the cards, we know full well that even the gloomiest of them, such as Death or the Devil, can represent good possibilities for change. You can therefore emphasize ways in which someone can aim to take back control of his or her life, or change an attitude, or find constructive elements in difficult times and circumstances.

Be very cautious about pronouncing on such matters as physical illness, and never predict human death. It's not in our remit as responsible Tarot readers. Be careful too not to use a reading as a vehicle to deliver a few home truths to a person you know well. Yes, the cards might indeed emphasize that this person is bossy or greedy or indecisive. But if this happens, try to look at the bigger picture: what is this characteristic a part of, in terms of the person's outlook? Usually, extending our preconceptions in this way generates compassion and understanding, and then the desire to make a point about their behavior simply melts away.

ACCEPTING PAYMENT FOR READINGS

Should you read cards for money? This is a decision everyone has to make for themselves. Personally, I do not accept payment. For the reasons just set out, I feel that reading the cards is dependent upon knowledge that I do not own, but is rooted in the spirit of the moment, which I do not engender. I have given my time, and some effort, to make the reading, but I am recompensed by the experience of doing it. Nor do I want to be bound to the terms of a commercial service, where the money must be equated with the value of the goods provided. I can't guarantee the results. Many people do read the Tarot professionally, and I won't argue with their choice. But in the tradition I have followed, we pass on knowledge as best we can without looking for financial gain.

This is a complex issue, and there can be situations where time and effort do equate to earning: giving talks, writing books, or teaching formal classes on Tarot are all situations where one would usually expect to be paid. In the case of the Tarot, I strongly recommend that you think through the implications of taking money for giving actual readings and make an informed decision. Set your own code of practice, and maintain your own sense of ethics in connection with the Tarot, and you'll steer a true course.

A middle way is to ask for something in exchange for a reading. A simple donation to the occasion or the room you meet in is a nice touch: a cake to share afterward or a plant for your sitting room would also do well. Feel free to make suggestions so that the other person has some idea of what would be appropriate. A bottle of wine, a book, or a travel day pass could be other options—something without too much monetary value but that will add to one's quality of life. This can lift a sense of obligation on behalf of the querents and helps them to realize that effort does go into the reading.

PREDICTION

Last, but by no means least, there is the vexed question of whether "prediction" is possible or advisable. You might think that this would come first in the considerations because divination usually involves some kind of forecasting. It is a is a tricky issue; for thousands of years theologians, philosophers, and diviners have argued over the nature of the future and free will. Where can we take a stand on this? I cannot deliver an authoritative judgment here, but I suggest that if you are drawn to Tarot, or indeed any form of divination practice, you already accept the idea of looking ahead, as well as at the past and the present. So unless you want to sharpen your wits by arguing your case with the naysayers, I recommend that you focus instead on the philosophy implicit within the cards and the Fool's Mirror layout as an integrated emblem of past, present, and future. Divisions of time may not have such tight boundaries as we tend to think. And to put this into practice, making sure that any prognostication doesn't sound too fateful, you can focus on the future cards as indicators of *what may happen if the current situation is allowed to develop in the way that it's going now.* The outcome as witnessed in the cards may therefore not be inevitable.

As a guideline, in the context of a reading, you can try to get a sense of what is more or less fixed and implicit within the situation, as opposed to what can be moderated by choice. For instance, the reading may reveal that the querent's father is acting obstructively (the Devil combined with the Emperor in relevant "external" positions could indicate this) but that if the querent is gentle but firm with the father (having Strength in an "internal" position could indicate this), this could be ameliorated. Then the consequences will change.

THE WAY IT WORKS

According to the way I was taught, the vagaries of human existence are a mixture of four factors: Fortune, Fate, Destiny, and Necessity. They are a kind of hierarchy that denote, in ascending order, the ways in which life is *not* entirely random. It's not really our job, as Tarot readers, to decide conclusively which of these forces is present in a reading, but sometimes we may get a strong sense of how one or more of them is acting in the situation. Here are some suggestions about how to handle this, but remember that we should all be cautious about how we interpret and communicate our perceptions in this respect.

Fortune

Fortune, or Luck, is part of our human lot. "Sometimes you win, sometimes you lose; the Wheel of Fortune turns" could be the motto for Lady Fortuna as she turns her handle. Both querent and reader need to accept that we all undergo fluctuations in this respect. However, we can perhaps help Fortune along a little sometimes; accentuating the positive can generate a mood of well-being that in turn may encourage a querent to embrace good fortune rather than ignoring its possibility. My Tarot teacher Glyn often bid us farewell by saying, "Be lucky!"

Fate

Fate may often be seen as embodied in a particular meeting, event, or accident that changes the course of our lives, for better or worse. "The hand of fickle, firking Fate" is another saying that I attribute to Glyn, who had a ready fund of quirky idioms up his sleeve. Perhaps some elements of our life are fated. "It was meant to be" is often voiced when such occurrences take place. However, perhaps even fate can sometimes be averted or ameliorated in the case of a potentially unwelcome event, as just indicated in the section on prediction. It is not necessarily the job of the Tarot reader to decide what is and isn't Fate at work in the spread of the cards, but it is very much a part of the Fool's Mirror approach to consider how we, or the querent in this case, can accept some responsibility for life's course, and to see what element of choice might be present in the workings of Fate.

Destiny

Destiny can represent the role or path that someone is born to take on; but embracing one's destiny may also be an act of conscious choice. We could say, for example, that Winston Churchill was a man of destiny in stepping into his role to lead the people of Great Britain through World War II. A destiny suggests a destination and something that we will grow into and develop a connection with as time progresses. Perhaps, as Tarot reader, you see a really important opportunity coming up for the querent; you can't make that person's choice for them if destiny is involved, but you can alert them to its presence.

Necessity

Necessity is when you can do nothing different. Force majeure is another way of describing it; again, it can be a happy or a fearful thing to contemplate, though in the moment of accepting the necessity of doing something, there is usually clarity and a sense of alignment with what must be, rather than any anxiety. Those who have experienced a serious accident often report that at the moment it happened they felt absolutely no fear. Again, we cannot know the ultimate workings of necessity, and it isn't always possible to judge for others when it is operating. If you consider that there really isn't a choice in the situation, then one way to tackle this is to say gently, "I think you may have to do such and such" as an indication that Necessity is operating here.

FOOL'S MIRROR DIVINATION

To round off this chapter, here's a set of key points that are intrinsic to the Fool's Mirror method in terms of managing the Tarot reading:

♣ Take on the tasks of setting up the space in which the reading will take place and of managing the course of the reading.

♣ Approach the Fool's Mirror spread as a whole, and look for detail, dynamics, and direction within that.

♣ Take responsibility for the reading, but recognize that the outcome doesn't entirely depend upon you or your powers.

♣ Deliver the reading as your own interpretation without attributing it to any other person, force, or spirit.

✤ Close the reading properly, and be ready to leave it behind.

✤ Consider the ethics involved in giving a reading, and pay attention to issues such as confidentiality, consideration for the client's feelings, and the question of remuneration or exchange of gifts.

I wish you many fruitful and interesting readings to come.

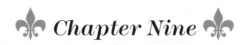 *Chapter Nine*

THE FOOL LEADS US FURTHER

The Fool is the wild card. Just when we think we have everything sorted in terms of our Tarot practice, he bounds in with a crazy idea, a new insight, a tempting trail to research. Tangents are his stock-in-trade, and he frequently reminds us that nothing is as fixed as we might have hoped. As the Fool can break into the sequence of the twenty-one cards, turning up amongst them wherever he pleases, so too can he symbolize the moment when we see things differently and realize that we don't have to stay locked into one set of assumptions. The Fool's Mirror flashes and catches our attention; it's time to take stock and head off in a new direction.

We would be wise to heed the Fool. Any system can become stultifying if it is taken as being fixed and immutable. Even a symbolic sequence as fluid as the Tarot can be imprisoning if our view of it becomes fossilized. The temptation can then be to layer on more attributions or to devise ever more complex schemes of correspondences. But although attributions and correspondences with other systems of knowledge can be very useful, they are a secondary level of information. Our primary connection with Tarot is by absorbing the images themselves, and renewing this process will help to keep our understanding fresh and our divination skills versatile.

In this final chapter, therefore, I put forward some approaches to further our creativity with Tarot and enrich our vision of the Triumphs. These exercises are not just for beginners, but can be fruitful at any stage of the game. It's a tribute to the richness of Tarot symbolism that we can return to it over and over again and always find something new and rewarding.

The exercises are reasonably self-explanatory and are not a graded program as such. This means you can do them as and when you wish; but by all means, go through them systematically if you prefer. I have indicated where it is better to complete the full sequence of a particular exercise. It can help to set aside time to work on some of the exercises, but others, as you will see, can be kept in mind while going about your daily business.

You will need a deck of Marseilles-type Tarot cards to carry out these exercises; working with images on a page is not enough here.

In line with the Fool's Mirror approach to Tarot, I offer all of these ideas in the spirit of exploration, following the Fool in his wanderings along the highways and byways. You never know where a new path will lead.

BRINGING TAROT TRIUMPHS TO LIFE

This first set of exercises helps to develop a strong connection with the life of the Tarot cards through their sensory qualities.

Sound and Movement

Take a card from anywhere in the pack. What sound or sounds do you hear? What kind of movement, if any, is taking place to generate these sounds? Imagine that this card is alive, and hear what is happening. Keep the characters within the same scene, but allow them a chance to move around a little and enact their role. Make notes afterward about what you discover.

Examples

These are just some of the sounds that could be generated by the cards; you may find you hear entirely different ones when you approach the cards in question.

- ♣ **Temperance**—water flowing, the quality of sound and volume varying as the jugs are tilted and rebalanced. The breeze creates a faint rustling in the angel's wings.

- ♣ **The Sun**—children's laughter as the twins play under the beams of the sun.

- ♣ **The Magician**—he deftly moves his paraphernalia; the dice rattle and the cups being replaced on a wooden table sound hollow.

Listen attentively to these sounds with your inner ear. They can create a powerful sense of presence for the card. Some sounds may be chilling, like the swish of Death's scythe, for instance, and some may be dramatic, such as the crack of lightning as it strikes the Tower, followed by a rumble and clatter of stones.

If there is no obvious sound, consider the nature of the silence. How does the quality of that silence vary from card to card? There may be silence between sounds too, as in the pause before you hear the High Priestess turn another page in her book. What could that silence signify?

Your own set of sounds will add to your personal interpretation of the cards. Just listen and allow yourself to hear what is going on.

Other Sensory Connections

Sound is a very powerful sense in helping us to connect to the individual cards, but there are other ways of doing this too. Let's take a look at the clothing, color, equipment, and light in the cards.

Clothing

What clothing do the figures in the Trumps wear? Of course, their appearance may vary a little between different packs, but that doesn't matter. Imagine that you are feeling the fabric between your fingers. You may find that the materials of individual garments seem very different to this touch even if they look similar. Imagine that you gently touch the hair or skin, or run your fingers through the fur of animal pelts. Note your own reaction: is there anything that you shudder to touch or long to stroke?

Every card contains living beings that can yield sensory information. Take note of anything else that happens as you touch; perhaps the character or creature will react, move, or even speak to you. Don't be surprised if you have an intense response to one or two aspects of the cards, but treat it as part of the range of experience rather than becoming overly concerned about what it means.

I recommend trying this out with no more than two or three cards at a time. It would be exhausting and counterproductive to go through the whole pack in one sitting;

keep the experience vivid by limiting its scope. It's perfectly possible to work this exercise with the whole pack in several sessions, but it is not essential to do so. Trying it out with, say, half a dozen cards on two separate occasions can create a strong impression and will help to trigger your innate sensory connection with other cards as you use them for divination or contemplation.

The effects of this exercise may be enlivening, or even electrifying, but do not give them too much permanent importance. They help us get to know the life of the Tarot cards, but they are not necessarily a pointer to fixed interpretations. Again, making notes is useful, and it can be enlightening to file them away for a few months before reading them with fresh eyes. Not only are there likely to be details you have forgotten, but you may find that new associations are sparked off from what you have written, bursting into life like sparks from a smoldering coal.

Color

As the color range varies in different decks, we can't analyze its significance or consider it to be an intrinsic part of each Tarot Triumph. Nevertheless, color is an important trigger in helping us to link to the cards. In your pack of cards, what do you think about the combinations of color? Which colors dominate, and which are used sparingly? Do you have another pack to compare them with?

I became used to the predominantly red, blue, and yellow of the Grimaud Marseilles pack. Then I was fascinated to discover another traditional Marseilles pack where the emphasis was on green and yellow, combined with a light mulberry shade instead of bright red. For a while I found it particularly refreshing to use this pack after years with the Grimaud one. Now, I like them both equally—and I've gained further inspiration by poring over digital images of a whole range of historic packs, marveling, for instance, at some with a strong indigo theme. Color can bring out different responses in us, and it may provide a special lift to a jaded imagination from time to time. Find out what color palettes you prefer and what your responses are to the various colors in your pack.

Equipment

Take note of what equipment is in the cards. There are plenty of implements: jugs, staffs, shields, a book, a knife, wheels, a wand, an arrow, and so on. What are they all for? What's their function? It might sound simple, but if you discern the intrinsic nature of a tool or instrument, you may understand more about its purpose and place in the card. Is it for support, for cutting through, for balancing, for directing, or for containing, perhaps? Keep in mind that the appearance of each item may differ in other Tarot decks. What is important is to get to the principle and purpose of the implement or object.

Light

What kind of light do you think illuminates each Tarot Triumph? We have obvious examples in the Star, the Moon, and the Sun: what are the qualities and properties of the light contained in those images? Where there is no obvious type of light, ask yourself how you imagine it to be. Is the scene set indoors or outdoors, for instance? Is it bright, clouded, or dim light? Again, these impressions need not become fixed in your mind for all time, but they will help you to detect the mood and atmosphere of the scene. A further consideration could be shadows: do you expect to find shadows in the images, or are they perhaps more like stage scenes, visions, or the stuff of legend, where there may be no shadows at all?

If you succeed in completing this first set of exercises with every Triumph, you will have come a long way toward knowing each one as a living symbol.

THE TRIUMPHS AS GUIDING IMAGES

An effective way to deepen our connection with the images on the cards is to work through the pack taking one Triumph at a time and living with it for a day. Completing this exercise will therefore take the better part of a month, allowing for a few days off here and there. But it doesn't have to be hard or disrupt your way of life. Simply set out the card of the day when you get up, spend a few minutes contemplating it, then keep it in mind for the rest of the day. Act, speak, and function as usual. It doesn't matter if the card goes to the back of your mind, and in fact it's better that way—don't make it an intense act of visualization. Just be aware that, for instance, "Today is Wheel of Fortune day."

Finish off the exercise at the end of each day, preferably just before you go to bed. Acknowledge the card and put it away. If you have significant dreams afterward you can jot them down the next morning. But don't try to hold on to anything during the night.

Insights about the nature of the card may come to you during the day too. Write those down if you can, or make a mental note and record them later. You may be surprised how synchronicities can crop up, linking the day's experiences to the qualities of the cards. I decided to refresh my connection with the cards by doing this exercise myself while writing this book, and during my progression through the images I noted quite a number of these symbolic occurrences. The day I was studying the Tower, for instance, part of my tooth broke off, causing a jagged rift rather like that of lightning rupturing the Tower. The day I was pondering Temperance, I happened to visit a water mill and found myself listening to the sound of water going through a millrace, another kind of controlled outpouring. You could argue that one can find associations in the external world with whatever card is chosen for that day. Perhaps this is true; but even if they are not always startling coincidences, we can use what life throws up to help illuminate the spirit of the cards.

It's possible that a card could become a personal guide or teacher for the day. You might feel a special affinity with one card in particular, or find that it prompts a deep emotional response. If that happens, accept this deeper level of contact, and write down what you learn or discover, but continue with the other cards and consider them as equals. It's important to maintain a connection with all twenty-two Triumphs and to know them as a whole.

Recommendations for this exercise:

* Wait until you are familiar with the pack as a whole and have had some practice in divination before you attempt it.

* Go through the pack in order. It's up to you, though, where you choose to place the Fool.

* It doesn't matter if you miss a day or two here and there—it happens! But aim to complete the whole exercise, one card per day, within a calendar month. Otherwise, it will tend to drag on.

* Keep in mind the difference between the image of the card in your mind and the external world. Don't try

to place the image in the external world, like a vision or hallucination.

✦ Make notes about your experience with each card before you move on to the next one. These could be ideas, images, observations, thoughts, or experiences. The wide range of your associations may surprise you.

✦ Keep the attention on the image light during the day; give your external life priority, and if you forget about it for a while, that's fine. Trust the unconscious to do its work.

✦ Do round off at the end of the day, and draw a line under your notes and under your mental participation.

✦ Aim to do all twenty-two cards for this particular exercise, since this way you will arrive at a balanced relationship with all twenty-two, and you will be better placed to understand that they *are* a set.

✦ It is possible, however, to single out a card or two for special treatment if it has been eluding or puzzling you in interpretations. This could be an ongoing technique where you decide to give the Emperor, or the Chariot, or the Star, for instance, a day of observation. That is best done as part of your ongoing Tarot practice once you know the cards well.

GETTING CREATIVE WITH TAROT

Some years ago, I was asked to contribute a story to an anthology called *Tarot Tales*. These were to be fictional stories whose basis or theme involved using Tarot cards. For my effort, I drew five cards at random from the pack to use as a basis for my story. I picked them out unseen, as you would for a reading, and allowed the images to stir my imagination. The cards I turned up were Temperance, Justice, Death, the Moon, and Strength, and the result was "The Ship of Night," a tale about a nocturnal excursion that began as a walk through the city to cure sleeplessness, then became a moonlight cruise, and ended with a lucky escape from a ferry that takes us over the watery border into the realm of death.[1] I wasn't sure if I could complete the story, as I don't regularly write fiction, but to my surprise the cards acted as a portal into another world where a fantasy came gliding into view.

I would recommend this exercise to anyone who enjoys writing. To prompt your imagination, it is probably best to pick cards at random and allow them to stimulate your creativity, rather than having certain ones in mind already. At first I wasn't pleased with the set that I drew, but on accepting them I found that they began to weave a story of their own. The number of cards need not always be five, but it's important to consider how many would be suitable. As we discovered earlier, three cards is the minimum needed to create a situation, but to compose a story, I think it is better to use more. Four as a number can imply conflict, which, as my English literature teacher used to say, is the essence of drama; but it can also mean a fixed position or gridlock. Five offers more versatility and scope for resolution as well as conflict, so this is what I recommend for a short story. Putting it simply, every story needs a situation, but also something must happen, change must occur, and a resolution or realization should be reached at the conclusion. If you can handle the slightly greater complexities of using six or seven cards, this might also open up interesting possibilities for the shaping of a story. The field is yours to explore.

Setting Up the Exercise

To start your story, make the moment of drawing the cards special. Here is one suggested way of doing this:

* Choose your time, either by deciding in advance when you are going to pick your cards or by recognizing a good moment when it comes along.

* Start by focusing on where you are sitting. Feel the weight of your body and check your position on the chair or floor.

* Sense your breath connecting with the whole space around you in whatever way comes naturally.

* See the wholeness of the room or location, as well as its detail; keep the attention wide.

* When you are ready, formulate your intention. It can be very simple, such as, "I am going to write a story." Speak it aloud, or let it resound in your mind. Keep the words clear and do not add to them or alter them as you pronounce them.

* Pick up the pack of the Major Arcana, shuffle it, and select your cards. You can fan out the deck and pick one card at a time, or you can spread the cards out on a surface—facedown, of course—and choose them from there.

* Wait until you have your chosen number of cards before you turn them faceup.

* Lay the cards out in the order that you drew them, but feel free to form different patterns to generate ideas.

The Writing Process

Let your thoughts and imagination do the rest. As a seasoned writer, I recommend that you don't start the actual writing process until you have gathered your ideas. It doesn't matter how random or fragmented they seem; just allow them to emerge. And if you don't get a clear idea for an actual story straightaway, keep hold of your notes and go back and have another session with the same cards later. It can be more fruitful to spend twenty minutes at a time over three sessions than to force yourself to stare at the cards for an hour. Allow the process to take its own natural time, but do keep checking in with the cards and your notes, otherwise you may lose sight of the project altogether.

When you are ready, start to write. Keep the cards displayed on view somewhere so that you can look at them for fresh inspiration if you need to.

When you have finished your first draft, put your writing away for at least a few days. Then come back to it, reread with fresh eyes, and edit what you've written.[2]

Music, Poetry, Painting, and Dance

There are many possibilities for using Tarot cards in creative endeavors, in all sorts of genres. Here are some ideas to kick-start your own creations:

♣ Write a song for a selected Tarot card, or perhaps contrasting ones for three different Trumps.

♣ Choose an appropriate musical instrument (or electronic sound) to represent each Tarot Trump, and, if possible, use some of these to improvise music based on your impressions of the cards.

♣ Set up a group of five to seven cards and write a dialogue or even a short play involving all of them. What would they argue about? What might they do together?

- Draw or paint a scene based on one of the Triumphs, but not a close copy of the image on the card. Develop your own interpretation.

- Experiment with movements or a dance for a few or even all of the Tarot cards.

- Write a poem for some or each of the cards. Try putting words into the mouths of the figures or symbols on the cards, so that the poems are written in the first person. For instance, the Sun could speak to the children, and the figure falling from the Tower could cry out his reactions to the experience.

- Make versions of the objects found in the cards—for example, a jug, a wand, or a shield. You could use any materials, such as clay or feathers, wood or textiles. Let your imagination play with the images, and develop color, touch, and texture from your impressions.

Some of these projects could be very enjoyable and stimulating as part of group work if you have the chance to get together with others interested in Tarot-themed activities.

ADDING TO YOUR STORE

There are also more structured and information-based ways to advance your studies. The most important thing is to develop your own core connection with the Tarot Triumphs as seeds sown in the soul, watered with a little history and context. And it will always be a case, if you want to be a Tarot practitioner, of keeping a balance between that living bond with Tarot and the influx of information from external sources. You may find that at times you are hungry for further input, whereas in some phases you prefer to stay with your own contemplations. For the times when you wish to study more, here are some suggestions for how you could do this.

Historical Discussion

There are a number of good Tarot forums online. While you may have to sift through some lengthy debates, they sometimes have very valuable references and discussions. Our knowledge of the possible historical sources for the Tarot cards is expanding all the time; the research is at an exciting stage of development, so I do recommend at least dipping into this on occasion.

Attributions

Tarot can be aligned with other systems, such as astrology or the kabbalistic Tree of Life. It falls outside the scope of this book to investigate these things here, but it is something you might wish to look into. Bear in mind that there is no single agreed-upon, objective way of doing this; there is no evidence as yet that the Tarot Triumphs were designed to accord with another system, and it may be that your version turns out to be as good as anyone else's. An acquaintance of mine who was both a Kabbalist and a Tarot reader once said that you could place the twenty-two cards any way you liked on the twenty-two paths of the Tree of Life and it would still make sense! I tend to agree with this. Attributions can be useful, and they help us to understand the relationship between different systems, but they shouldn't become a straightjacket.

There is nothing to stop you from developing a method of aligning Tarot to your own area of interest, whether it be theosophy, psychotherapy, meditation, or homeopathy. This could be a way to enrich both practices. The important thing to keep in mind is that no one system of correspondences is the final authority; be honest with yourself if you can see that they don't accord in certain ways. No set of correspondences aligns two systems exactly—if it did, the systems would be the same in the first place.

Tarot Imagery

There are some wonderful resources online for studying historic Tarot packs. This is a banquet both for those who like to analyze the fine detail of the cards and for those who just wish to gaze at the images. In my experience, the British Museum leads the way with something like 250 listings of old Tarot cards, mostly in sets, though not all complete. The majority of these are digitized images that you can not only view on screen but also order as free downloadable jpgs for private research (copyright terms apply to all other usage).

Layouts

If you are confident in using the layouts for card readings, you could also consider devising a layout of your own. This is a path that others have trodden, so I can't pretend it's an original idea; one of my correspondents refers to a book that contains 122 layouts![3] Some layouts are designed with particular packs in mind, or for use with the entire Tarot deck of seventy-eight cards, including minor suits. If you wish to create a design for the Major Trumps only, your options may be more limited— but also, perhaps, more interesting. Consider the following questions and suggestions:

♣ How many cards can you viably use in the layout? Could you devise another type of layout to use all twenty-two? Or, if you prefer to use fewer cards, what is the maximum number that would have signifi-cance within that framework? For example, if there are more than eleven, then each card is more likely to turn up than not.

✤ Will you incorporate a time frame for past, present, and future?

✤ Do you want to designate areas of life for your read-ing, for instance for money, love, or family? The twelve astrological houses can be a good basis for this.

✤ Will you have a significator? If so, will this represent the person concerned, the specific situation, or could it be either one?

✤ What pattern or geometric shape will be embedded in your spread? Could you do, perhaps, an eight-pointed star, or a lightning flash zigzag? What significance would this have?

✤ Will your divination procedure include any special points? For example, in the Fool's Mirror layout, the presence of the Fool in the central line shows that the reading is blocked.

✤ Try to give your layout a name that reflects its sym-bolic or legendary qualities.

Do give your divination layout a few practice runs, and don't be afraid to make alterations based on these.

THE FOOL'S MIRROR FOR THE FUTURE

As we reach the end of this book, I would like to wish you all the best with your Tarot practice. Whether you use Tarot for divination, personal illumination, or creative inspiration, it is an interest that can last a lifetime. We learn, develop, and pass on our knowledge, as it is my intention to do here. My own curiosity drew me to the Tarot, and I discovered an innate affinity with it, but I owe much to the Tarot masters who have helped me along the way. I hope that some of the concepts expressed here will do justice to what I have learned from others and that this exposition of the Fool's Mirror method will help in some way to further the life of the Tarot, a remarkable set of symbols and way of knowledge that we have been fortunate enough to inherit.

ACKNOWLEDGMENTS

Many thanks to Richard Smoley and Tony James for reading drafts of this text and making valuable suggestions. This helped me more than they probably realized in setting the book on the right track. And I warmly thank my agent, Doreen Montgomery, as always, for her unfailing support and encouragement. Most especially, I thank my husband, Robert Lee-Wade, for taking on the task of creating exquisite line drawings of the Tarot cards to accompany this book. This was time out from his usual art of painting in oils, but it fulfilled a dream that we had when we first met on board a ship that one day we would create a book together.

NOTES

CHAPTER ONE:
Enter the Triumphs

1 Various Tarot historians have acknowledged the partial association of Tarot cards with late medieval and Renaissance processions. A good description of the tradition can be found in Robert Place, *The Tarot: History, Symbolism and Divination* (New York: Tarcher, 2005), 109–25.

CHAPTER TWO:
The Tarot as a Method of Divination

1 My childhood version goes: "Who will I marry? Tinker, tailor, soldier, sailor, rich man, poor man, beggar man, thief. What will I be dressed in? Silk, satin, cotton, rags. How will I get to the wedding? Coach, carriage, wheelbarrow, dustcart . . ." The rest is lost in the mists of memory, and so the oral tradition goes on.

2 *The Zohar* Book IV, trans. Harry Sperling and Maurice Simon (London: The Soncino Press, 1933), 143. *The Zohar* is a collection of mystical writings on the

Kabbalah that first appeared in Spain in the thirteenth century.

3 Other cultures may attribute the source of divination responses to a particular deity, angel, the power of the ancestors, or nature. While this is a fascinating topic, it would take us too far away from the direction of this book to explore it further.

4 "Lilly's 'Fish Stolen' judgement, dated 10th February 1638 and given as an example chart in *Christian Astrology*, is a horary masterpiece." David Plant, "The Life & Work of William Lilly," Skyscript.co.uk, last accessed March 10, 2016, *www.skyscript.co.uk/ lilly.html*.

5 An account of Lilly's interpretation and detective work can be found at *www.astrologiaoraria.com/ frawley2Eng.html* or in Lilly's casebook, known as *Christian Astrology* or *An Introduction to Astrology*, available online (but without horoscope charts) at *sacred-texts.com/astro/aia/index.htm*. The book appears in various editions and formats; in mine (*An Introduction to Astrology* [Hollywood, CA: Newcastle Publishing, 1972]), the case is set out in the chapter on Seventh House astrology.

6 I remember reading an interview with Sir Laurens van der Post (1906–1996) in which he said that at the christening of Prince William, where he became the prince's godfather, there was a sudden storm, causing one of the baptismal candles to flicker violently. The flame nearly went out, but it recovered. Sir Laurens van der Post interpreted this to mean that the British monarchy would come under severe threat but would reestablish its position with the

British people. This was some years before the death of Princess Diana and the subsequent cloud that seriously dimmed the popularity of the monarchy for a period.

7 Ronald Decker, *The Esoteric Tarot: Ancient Sources Rediscovered in Hermeticism and Cabalah* (Wheaton, IL: Quest Books, 2013), 60.

8 Place, *The Tarot*, 17.

9 For an in-depth discussion of the last two meanings, see Michael S. Howard's article, "From 'Barocchi' to 'Tarocchi': The Evolution of the Term 'Barocco' into 'Tarocco,'" Le Tarot Cultural Association, translated February 2014, *www.letarot.it/page.aspx?id=429&lng=ENG*.

10 My knowledge of Russian traditional culture was acquired over many years and a multitude of trips to Russia, during which time I researched Russian folk art and folklore. *Russian Magic*, published by Quest in 2009, was one successful outcome. My Russian Tarot cards are based on Russian folklore and nature spirits.

11 Further information about the triumphal processions and Petrarch's *Triumphs* can be found in Place, *The Tarot*, 111–25.

12 As Ronald Decker points out in *The Esoteric Tarot*, "In the very period when both the archetypal Tarot and allegorical art were most familiar, viewers complained that the trumps were a senseless mishmash. This reaction is an important clue. It disqualifies certain modern theories that base the trumps' symbolism primarily on some famous literary work,

be it the Apocalypse of St. John or the poetry of Petrarch" (8–9).

13 A study published in 2012 has been widely reported in the media. See, for example, Stephanie Pappas, "Origin of the Romani People Pinned Down," *Live-Science*, December 6, 2012, *www.livescience.com/25294-origin-romani-people.html*; and Giles Tremlett, "Gypsies Arrived in Europe 1,500 Years Ago, Genetic Study Says," *The Guardian*, December 7, 2012, *www.theguardian.com/world/2012/dec/07/gypsies-arrived-europe-1500-genetic*.

14 See Marjorie Rowling, *Everyday Life of Medieval Travellers* (New York: Dorset Press, 1989), 90–97.

CHAPTER THREE:
Taking on the Tarot

1 When I was studying traditional Russian arts and crafts, I visited one of the longest-running matry-oshka, or Russian nesting doll, workshops at Semy-onov. The dolls were painted with very simple designs without a great deal of variation, but the women artists were at pains to explain that every face on the dolls was important to them. They wanted each face to look kind. They were also proud to explain the simple symbols on the dolls—birds for happiness, flowers for beauty, and so on. Their artistic role in the creation of the dolls was not highly skilled or imaginative, but they entered into it with good intent, to make something that had a presence and was not just a slavish reproduction. Something similar may have happened in the Tarot ateliers,

and many of the colorists could have taken just the same kind of approach.

2 In *The Tree of Life Oracle: Use the Sacred Wisdom of the Kabbalah to Enrich Your Life* (New York: Barnes & Noble, 2002), a divination system based on the kabbalistic Tree of Life, Gila Zur and I made minor changes to the original version, which was known as *Galgal*. We considered that this made the oracle more approachable and in keeping with a wider readership. Perhaps this is the first of more changes in the future.

3 Currently published by Heron, Maîtres-Cartier à Bordeaux and purchased via Amazon France.

4 See chapter eight, "Managing the Reading."

5 Robert Lee-Wade, my husband, is a Royal Ulster Academician specializing in oil painting. See *www .robertleewade.co.uk.*

6 See chapter six, "A Search for Order and Meaning in the Fool's Mirror."

7 See my book, *Stories from the Silk Road* (Cambridge, MA: Barefoot Books, 1999).

8 "The Sorcerer's Apprentice" was turned into a symphonic poem by the French composer Paul Dukas in 1896–1897. The music was also used in Walt Disney's film *Fantasia*. My father used to explain the story to me when I listened to the record as a child.

9 See the section in chapter nine on working with one card every day and noting your dreams during the process.

10 See chapter eight, "Managing the Reading."

CHAPTER FOUR:
The Wandering Fortune-Teller

1 The question of whether one should take payment for Tarot readings is fully discussed in chapter eight.

2 Gilchrist and Zur, *The Tree of Life Oracle.*

3 A phrase first coined by the poet Alexander Pope in his verses entitled "An Essay on Criticism" (1711), *http://www.poetryfoundation.org/learning/essay/237826.*

CHAPTER FIVE:
Becoming the Diviner—
Grasping the Fool's Mirror

1 Beatrice Otto, *Fools Are Everywhere: The Court Jester around the World* (Chicago: University of Chicago Press, 2001), 250.

2 It is relatively easy to find references and images for these packs online.

3 Otto, *Fools Are Everywhere*, 250.

4 Zero would not have been a natural attribution, as it was a latecomer to the European numbering system. The history of zero is contentious because it was invented in more than one place, but it was not much more than punctuation or a placeholder until it was developed in seventh-century India and then picked up in medieval Europe. Even then it was only associated with "darkly magical" practices. John Matson, "The History of Zero," Scientific American, August 21, 2009, *http://www.scientificamerican.com/article/history-of-zero/.*

5 And note that jongleurs were not exclusively male; there were also plenty of female jongleurs.

6 A similar occurrence is quoted in *The Wind on the Heath: A Gypsy Anthology*, ed. John Sampson (London: Chatto and Windus, 1930), as an anecdote of Sir Walter Scott. Scott also wrote that gypsy glamour is "the power of imposing on the eyesight of the spectators, so that the appearance of an object shall be totally different from the reality." Cited in Lewis Spence, *An Encyclopaedia of Occultism* (New York: Dodd, Mead, and Co., 1920), 198.

7 This has been pointed out by Ronald Decker in *The Esoteric Tarot* (see chapter two, note 8).

8 See Mary K. Greer, "Papess Maifreda Visconti of the Guglielmites—new evidence," November 7, 2009, *https://marygreer.wordpress.com/2009/11/07 /papess-maifreda-visconti-of-the-guglielmites%E2 %80%94new-evidence/* and Robert O'Neill, "Papess Cards," September 19, 2013, *http://www.tarot.com /tarot/robert-oneill/papess-cards*.

9 The Shekinah is the female spirit of grace, the feminine counterpart of the male creator, in Jewish and kabbalistic mysticism.

10 Decker, *The Esoteric Tarot*, 106 and 117.

11 It's possible that certain sets of cards may have allied the image with Pope Joan or Manfreda to make a particular point, or reference, but this would not be the main intention in depicting the High Priestess.

12 Decker, *The Esoteric Tarot*, 120.

13 I have seen two illuminations illustrating the text of *La Somme le Roy*, dating from the turn of the fourteenth century, which both show Prudence

as a crowned female figure instructing a crowd of respectful supplicants from a book or scroll. Prudence has been singled out as the cardinal virtue not present in the Tarot pack: Justice, Strength, and Temperance are all there. However, if these cardinal virtues do form a part of the Tarot structure—and this is debatable—then aligning the High Priestess to Prudence does make sense, and it completes the quadruplicity of virtues.

14 Waite's version of the Empress discards her authoritarian, official appearance and portrays her as Queen of Love, ruled by Venus.

15 The Sun and Moon cards are also candidates for this role. It is unlikely that the Tarot is based entirely on alchemy, but it is quite possible that allusions might have been made to the alchemical process.

16 The association of the eagles on the shields of the Empress and Emperor with the eagles of Zeus is emphasized in Place, *The Tarot*, 136. But sometimes the Empress's eagle is portrayed as a different type of bird altogether. Ronald Decker makes a case for identifying this as a vulture based on the use of the ancient Egyptian hieroglyph of a vulture to mean mother, something he suggests has been transmitted into the Tarot through Renaissance Hermetic philosophy (*The Esoteric Tarot*, 107).

17 The symbol of two birds facing one another is deeprooted in its own right and is often found in early Christian and Islamic art.

18 He may also represent beatitude as one of the highest virtues. See Decker, *The Esoteric Tarot*, 7, 131, 132.

19 In the Middle Ages, the link between pupil and master was considered highly important. Knowledge was passed down through the ranks with due respect shown to those further up the hierarchy. In the early medieval Arab schools, the great teacher would sit at the center of two or more concentric circles, with the most experienced students forming the inner circle and the novices on the outer periphery. It was the job of the older students to relay the teachings back to the younger ones.

20 See Mary K. Greer, "The Visconti Tarots," July 3, 2011, *https://marygreer.wordpress.com/2011/07/03/the-visconti-tarots/* and Mary Packard, *The Golden Tarot: The Visconti-Sforza Deck* (New York: Race Point Publishing, 2013), 60.

21 Robert Place also picks up on the significance of Pythagoras's Y-shaped choice in relation to the Lover (*The Tarot*, 124–5).

22 As in the Tarot of Pierre Madénie, Dijon, 1709.

23 "Late medieval and early Renaissance literature and art frequently portrayed human-animal hybrids." Simona Cohen, *Animals as Disguised Symbols in Renaissance Art* (Leiden, The Netherlands: Brill, 2008), 222.

24 Lions were also associated with the ancient Phrygian goddess Cybele, whose cult was popular later in Rome; she was said to represent the Great Mother.

25 To these four cardinal virtues are often added the three theological or heavenly virtues of faith, hope, and charity, forming a set of seven virtues, which are the counterpart to the seven deadly sins.

26 Those who wanted such a conventional or straightforwardly recognizable set of emblems had the

Minchiate Tarot to work with. Although this contains similar cards to the twenty-two Triumphs of the Marseilles Tarot, it has been expanded to include sets of images representing, for instance, the signs of the zodiac, the theological virtues, the four elements, and the five senses. It is much more schematic, but although it is overtly more philosophical, it seems to have been used primarily as a card game rather than for illumination or divination. See *A History of Playing Cards and a Bibliography of Cards and Gaming* by Catherine Perry Hargrave (Mineola, NY: Dover, 1966), 228–9 and indexed references.

27 In the thirteenth century, the Eremiti Augustini order of hermits was formed, evolving into companies of friars.

28 It could be difficult to survive as a solitary; the mystic Jan van Ruysbroeck (c. 1293–1381) had to get official permission to take over a forest hermitage near Brussels so that he could live there peacefully with his followers. Unfortunately, the local nobles took advantage of the hermit's obligation to provide spiritual and physical succor and descended too often in their hunting parties to strip the larder bare, so Ruysbroeck had to place his community under the rule of St. Augustine in order to continue the contemplative life without intrusion.

29 See Rowling, *Everyday Life of Medieval Travellers*, 135–39, where the author reveals fascinating details of the hermit's life, including the efforts of a Provençal eremite called Bénézet to raise funds for the building of the famous bridge at Avignon. Robert M. Place cites hermits as entirely solitary ascetics

(*The Tarot*, 142), but history shows that their role was often more complex.

30 I noted this allusion to Diogenes many years ago and now find that Robert Place (*The Tarot*, 143) also confirms this as a likelihood, citing Diogenes and the lantern as a common emblem in the Renaissance.

31 See Place, *The Tarot*, 141–2.

32 Although there is still speculation as to how much certain artifacts are records of lunar cycles and sometimes star positions, there seems to be overall agreement that very early tallies of this type were made. Lorna Simmons, "Ancient Time Keepers," University Lowbrow Astronomers at the University of Michigan, June 1999, *http://umich.edu/~lowbrows /reflections/1999/lsimmons.2.html*.

33 From "Fortune Plango Vulnera," in *Carmina Burana*, a collection of eleventh- to thirteenth-century lyrics, mostly in Latin, popularized by the composer Carl Orff.

34 Rowling, *Everyday Life of Medieval Travellers*, 97.

35 Place, *The Tarot*, 149. As Place also points out, there is some evidence for this in that one or two packs do call the Hanged Man by the name of Traitor. However, there is also room in the history of Tarot for this to be a variant of the main meaning, rather than the original intention, especially since there is evidence to support the acrobat theory in the very early so-called Charles VI pack (fifteenth century), where he is shown holding bags that are very likely to be a gymnast's weights. A dead or dying man would not be able to hold anything while hanging upside-down.

36 Several accounts are given in Joseph Strutt, *The Sports and Pastimes of the People of England* (London: Methuen, 1801).

37 "The rope-dancing is performed by a woman holding a balancing pole; and on the same rope a man, probably 'clown to the rope,' is represented hanging." Quoted in Strutt, *The Sports and Pastimes of the People of England*, Book III, 188 and illustrated in *Orbis Pictus* by the Czech author Comenius, an encyclopedia for children that he wrote in 1658.

38 An account of the Tarlà can be found at *http:// gironablog.blogspot.co.uk/2008/05/some-girona-legends-tarl.html*. Judging by clips on YouTube, some live acrobats like to try to replicate his feats today too!

39 Death is usually personified as male in Western culture, although this is not a given, and in some cultures Death is seen as female. See *http://en.wikipedia .org/wiki/Death_%28personification%29*. See also Karl Siegfried Guthke, *The Gender of Death: A Cultural History in Art and Literature* (Cambridge: Cambridge University Press, 1999).

40 Revelation 6:8.

41 Charles Herbermann and George Williamson, "Dance of Death," *The Catholic Encyclopedia* 4 (New York: Robert Appleton Company, 1908), *http://www.newadvent .org/cathen/04617a.htm*. The article includes a fascinating account of this in a carnival procession in Northern Italy in the early era of Tarot cards. This includes a Last Judgment that we can recognise from the Tarot pack:

"In Florence (1559) the 'triumph of death' formed a part of the carnival celebration. We may describe it as follows: After dark a huge wagon, draped in black and drawn by oxen, drove through the streets of the city. At the end of the shaft was seen the Angel of Death blowing the trumpet. On the top of the wagon stood a great figure of Death carrying a scythe and surrounded by coffins. Around the wagons were covered graves which opened whenever the procession halted. Men dressed in black garments on which were painted skulls and bones came forth and, seated on the edge of the graves, sang dirges on the shortness of human life. Before and behind the wagon appeared men in black and white bearing torches and death masks, followed by banners displaying skulls and bones and skeletons riding on scrawny nags. While they marched the entire company sang the Miserere with trembling voices."

42 Curiously, Temperance in the fifteenth-century Visconti-Sforza pack has no liquid flowing from her jugs. She does wear a delightful pair of red socks though!

43 See Decker, *The Esoteric Tarot*, 109.

44 See the entry for Justice in this chapter.

45 See Place, *The Tarot*, 151. The four humors was a widespread conception in medieval and Renaissance times, with classical origins; it underpinned much of astrology and medicine and formed a popular psychology of the times. I do not think it is worth delving too far into this to understand Temperance in terms of the Tarot, as we need to see it more from a contemporary viewpoint in terms of interpretation, but it can be a useful reminder of the mix of meanings.

46 Popular illustrations of "monsters" who had reputedly been born to unfortunate women in early Renaissance Italy appear on broadsides and woodcuts circulated at the time. They were drawn in a manner very similar to the Tarot Devil, with the same improbable leathery wings, horns, and clawed feet and a curious combination of male, female, and animal characteristics. Such creatures were feared and perhaps comprehended as spawn of the Devil. See Ottavia Niccoli, *Prophecy and People in Renaissance Italy*, trans. Lydia G. Cochrane (Princeton University Press, 1990), 39–41.

47 See, for instance, "The False Knight on the Road" from the famous collection of British ballads. Here, the Devil tries to prevent a child from getting home, but the boy outsmarts the Devil by facing up to him and countering all his propositions. The tunes of this genre of song often go at a rollicking pace, suggesting that we must stay lively and a touch merry in order to outface the Devil.

48 See the illustration for "Orgeuil" (Pride) in *Somme le Roi*, British Museum Add MS 28162, dating from 1290–1300. This shows a king toppling from a tower, watched by three ladies.

49 Nicola McDonald, *Pulp Fictions of Medieval England: Essays in Popular Romance* (Manchester: Manchester University Press, 2004), 56.

50 "Three days after his consecration as bishop on 6 July 1984, York Minster was struck by lightning, resulting in a disastrous fire which some interpreted as a sign of divine wrath at Jenkins's appointment. As a bishop, Jenkins was known for his willingness to speak his mind." "David Jenkins (bishop)," Wikipedia,

last modified March 6, 2016, *http://en.wikipedia .org/wiki/David_Jenkins_%28bishop%29.*

51 Panels in the parish church of Widecombe-in-the-Moor, United Kingdom, commemorate a terrible lightning strike in 1638. The panels displayed there include the following pronouncement:

A crack of lightning suddenly, with thunder hail and fire

Fell on the church and tower here and ran into the choir;

A sulferous smell came with it, and the tower strangely rent,

The stones abroad into the air, with violence were sent.

Some broken small as dust or sand, some whole as they came out

From of the building and here lay, in places round about.

The poem goes on to marvel at how some folk were burned while others were completely spared by the lightning fire.

52 The best-known examples are at San Gimignano, Italy, originally built in the eleventh to fourteenth centuries as watchtowers. Later, each owner strove to improve his status by outdoing the others in terms of height.

53 We know that Isis was still celebrated as a symbol of female divinity up until Renaissance times, having been written up by Plutarch. Given that there is a link between Isis and Ishtar, and that Isis too penetrated the underworld to recover her lover Osiris, it's possible that this could also have been transmitted

through the centuries. However, in historical terms, it may be more likely that the general myth of a Star figure as Queen of the Heavens has infused this Tarot card. But again, it's possible that this emblem could represent a stage of initiation in some esoteric school. Freemasonry has a symbol known as the Blazing Star, or l'Etoile Flamboyante, which A. E. Waite draws attention to in his *Pictorial Key to the Tarot* in connection to the Star.

54 Visitors to Venice may be struck, too, by a resemblance of the towers in the Moon to those of the medieval Arsenal, which guards another watery domain, standing on either side of a major canal at the entrance to the sea lagoon in the Adriatic, in which the island-city lies. I have always found this an eerie, compelling place, which puts me in mind of the Tarot Moon.

55 A few early Tarot versions of the Moon are completely different: the Moon is held aloft by a young girl or youth, or associated with images of astronomers measuring her course. But the Marseilles version, with slight variations such as full face or profile Moon, soon became firmly established as the prime Tarot image. Was it therefore deliberately drafted with the intent of creating a more occult image? Or was it perhaps a kind of natural selection that discarded other versions and quickly established symbols that seemed more evocative?

56 See image at *http://www.britishmuseum.org/research /collection_online/collection_object_details.aspx? objectId=369364&partId=1*.

"The presence of the solar and lunar emblems, and the eight-pointed star of Venus at the head of the symbols on most of the boundary-stones suggests that an astral character underlies them." The author goes on to suggest that some of the accompanying symbols are taken from the zodiac. He also refers to the eight-pointed star as representing Venus, possibly another lead to the Star in the Tarot pack. L. W. King, *Babylonian Boundary-Stones and Memorial-Tablets in the British Museum* (London: Longmans, 1912).

57 The crayfish, it seems, was known in Europe from the Middle Ages onward, though it might have been a relatively new addition to the diet at that time. But they had already gained a reputation in ancient Greece: "Aristotle in ancient Greece knew about them roughly year 300 BCE. Crayfish were believed to have magic power. Thus ash from crayfish burned alive and a solution made from crayfish and alcohol was used against bites of snakes and stings of scorpions, sudden high fever or bites by dogs with rabies." Boris Grahn, "History of Crayfish," *http://www.crayfishworld.com/history.htm.* Perhaps we should also take into account that people of all eras are very confused about the differences between crayfish, lobsters, and even prawns, as indeed one academic paper points out. Emmanuil Koutrakis, Yoichi Machino, Dimitra Mylona, and Costas Perdikaris, "Crayfish Terminology in Ancient Greek, Latin, and Other European Languages," *Crustaceana* 0 (0): 1–12, DOI: 10.1163/001121609X12475745628586, *http://www.academia.edu/2539783/Crayfish_terminology_in_ancient_Greek_Latin_and_other_European_languages.*

58 Another kabbalistic allusion could be to the yods of divine light, which are sparked off by the first letter of the Hebrew name of God.

59 This image of a boy on horseback in conjunction with the Sun appears only once in traditional Marseilles packs, to my knowledge, in the rather quirky Vieville Tarot of 1650. It is thought to be the inspiration for the Sun in the contemporary Rider-Waite pack.

60 The Moon also shows signs of being a cosmic clock in some early representations. Robert M. Place emphasizes the timekeeping function of the Sun and the Moon, along with an alliance to Fate (*The Tarot*, 159).

61 See Peter Gelling and Hilda Ellis Davidson, *The Chariot of the Sun and Other Rites and Symbols of the Northern Bronze Age* (London: J. M. Dent, 1969), 176–9. This is discussed in the section called "The Twins" as part of an archaeological and historical survey of sun symbolism. They mention folk customs for kindling new fire in countries such as Serbia, Bulgaria, and Bohemia, where two brothers or twins would strip themselves naked to kindle the flame.

62 I can't help thinking that if we could find a similar contemporary representation of two little half-naked boys standing in front of a wall then we would be closer to establishing the immediate source of the Tarot card image.

63 This isn't exclusively a Christian doctrine; a Muslim Sufi teacher once told me that belief in both angels and judgment after death forms a common ground of faith between Islam and Christianity. Plus there is the Egyptian myth already referred to under Justice

where the soul passes through a judgment hall after death. Many other religious or mythical traditions also envisage a passage of trial for the human being entering the afterlife. A comprehensive description of Last Judgment beliefs and iconography in Christian, Islamic, and Judaic teachings is given at *http://en.wikipedia.org/wiki/Last_Judgment*.

64 *The Hymn of the Robe of Glory*, translated by G. R. S. Mead in 1908 and dating from early Christian Era. Available online at The Gnostic Society Library, *http://gnosis.org/library/grs-mead/grsm_robeofglory.htm*.

65 Gurdjieff quoted from the Gospel to show that this was not a new teaching (for instance, in the parable of the virgins and the bridegroom, Matthew 25, where the foolish virgins slept and the wise ones stayed awake to meet their lord) and declared that we need to heed the call to wake up in order to embrace our true potential. His own system involved what were at the time (early to mid 1900s) particularly innovative methods and tasks to shake people out of sleep and make them pay real attention to the world around them.

66 These represent the Gospel makers Matthew, Mark, Luke, and John and have been used in Christian iconography since the early centuries of the Christian era. They are derived from the Bible, the Book of Ezekiel, and the Revelation of St. John. John Vinycomb, "Emblems of the Four Evangelists," from *Fictitious and Symbolic Creatures in Art* (1909), *http://www.sacred-texts.com/lcr/fsca/fsca13.htm*.

67 Though of course, this does not mean that it was not implied or contained within early myths and

philosophies, only that Plato is credited with first bringing it to public attention in a clearly defined form.

68 The overlap and shifting imagery to identify the different lines of thought are beyond the scope of this book, but Robert Fludd's well-known image of *Integra Naturae*, which he included in his third book, *Macrocosmus*, can be viewed at *http://farm7 .static.flickr.com/6187/6130074265_d9eee51380_ o.jpg*. For a more detailed exposition of the different sources of this image, see Place, *The Tarot*, 162.

69 The Chinese oracle the I-Ching is usually translated as The Book of Changes and is based on the changing positions of unbroken and broken lines within a series of hexagrams, six-line figures made up of these two variables and their transitional states through changing lines.

70 The mandorla is an almond shape generated by two overlapping circles and is commonly used to frame up holy images such as that of Christ.

CHAPTER SIX:
A Search for Order and Meaning in the Fool's Mirror

1 Astrology, of course, was taking the external reference points of the movements of the planets through the "fixed stars" (the band of the zodiac as defined by astrology), whereas Tarot, as far as we know, has no such objective external framework in mind. However, the challenge of developing meaningful symbols is similar in both cases, and this is allied to the underlying concepts of number, which Babylonian

and Greek astrologers developed over a lengthy period of time. For a detailed analysis of the early centuries of astrology, see Jack Lindsay, *The Origins of Astrology* (London: Frederick Muller, 1971).

2 It is beyond the scope of this book (and my own powers of explanation!) to go into the basis of number interpretation, but there are many good studies available. See, for instance, Keith Critchlow, *The Hidden Geometry of Flowers: Living Rhythms, Form and Number* (Edinburgh: Floris Books, 2011), which gives an excellent synthesis of how natural geometric forms ally to the principle of number and relate to philosophical interpretations of the universe.

3 I am very grateful to Ronald Decker for pointing this out (*The Esoteric Tarot*, 45); it is something that hadn't occurred to me before, and I hadn't come across a reference to it in any other Tarot context.

4 Remember that the Tarot suits contain one more court card than the suits of regular playing cards; there is a page as well as knight or jack, king, and queen.

5 I do of course respect the right of other authors to draw their own conclusions about the importance of Tarot numbers (for example, acclaimed Tarot specialist Rachel Pollack in *Seventy-Eight Degrees of Wisdom: A Book of Tarot* [San Francisco: Weiser Books, 1997]). However, I'd also suggest that developing full meanings for the seventy-eight cards is more profitable with a complete pictorial pack, such as the Rider-Waite pack, which she has used here.

6 For those who want to take it further, it could perhaps be analyzed as a Venn diagram, using the intersecting circles to illustrate the similarities,

differences, and relationships between groups—or in this case the three different circles. In this way, too, the Fool shares common ground with all the other cards but stands in his unique position, which goes well with his meaning.

7 A quick online search will reveal many images of the original Celtic crosses, which were often made in stone. For a basic discussion of the history and significance of the design, see *http://en.wikipedia .org/wiki/Celtic_cross*.

8 A. E. Waite (1857–1942) was a mystic and occultist who was a member of the Order of the Golden Dawn, a Freemason, and highly knowledgeable about Rosicrucianism, Kabbalah, and ceremonial magic. He was a prolific author and also a publisher. Waite's evident concern for ethical approaches to magic and honoring the sacred gave him a particularly elevated stature among the esoteric ranks of the day.

9 R. A. Gilbert, a specialist in the work of A. E. Waite and the Order of the Golden Dawn, says that he has come across no evidence confirming the origins of the Celtic Cross Tarot spread, and writes: "It is tempting to assume that he derived it from the Golden Dawn, and from Florence Farr in particular, but there is no evidence at all to support the idea" (email to the author, April 7, 2015).

10 If you look at Web pages describing the layout and the interpretation of the positions, you will find other variations on Waite's original version. See, for example, *http://www.learntarot.com/ccross.htm*, and *http:// www.biddytarot.com/how-to-read-the-celtic-cross-tarot-spread/*.

11 See the *Complete Book of Tarot Spreads*, which includes 122 layouts, by Evelin Burger and Johannes Fiebig (New York: Sterling Ethos, 2014).

CHAPTER SEVEN:
The Fool's Mirror Layout

1 This is similar to the way in which we consider the whole of the horoscope in astrology, where every planet plays its part, and even the "untenanted" signs of the zodiac, with no planets in them, still have significance in the reading of the chart. Although the astrologer will give most weight to the positions of the planets and their signs, the chart itself is an entity, and everything within it plays a part.

2 Sir Walter Scott, ed., *Hermetica: The Ancient Greek and Latin Writings which Contain Religious or Philosophic Teachings Ascribed to Hermes Trismegistus* (Boston: Shambala, 1993), book IV, section 4, 151.

3 See especially works by the biologist Rupert Sheldrake.

CHAPTER EIGHT:
Managing the Reading

1 See Cherry Gilchrist, *Russian Magic: Living Folk Traditions of an Enchanted Landscape*, (Wheaton, IL: Quest Books, 2009), 29.

2 Figure 12, *Book of Lambspring*, as in A. E. Waite's edition of 1893. This is an allegory of alchemy as a spiritual path; the caption to this emblem is: "Another mountain of India lies in the vessel / Which the spirit and the soul – / That is, the Son and the Guide – have climbed."

CHAPTER NINE:
The Fool Leads Us Further

1 Cherry Gilchrist, "The Ship of Night," in *Tarot Tales*, ed. Rachel Pollack and Caitlin Matthews (New York: Ace Books, 1996).

2 If you want to go further into the craft of story writing and editing, there are many good books available on the subject. For writing up your own memoirs, and a general approach to life writing, see my book *Your Life, Your Story: Writing Your Life Story for Family and Friends* (London: Piatkus, 2010). There is also another writing manual that I've come across that uses Tarot cards for writing exercises: Cathy Birch, *Awaken the Writer Within: A Sourcebook for Releasing Your Creativity and Finding Your True Writer's Voice* (Oxford: How To Books, 2005) 43–6.

3 Burger and Fiebig, *Complete Book of Tarot Spreads*; email correspondence with Byron Zeliotis.

GLOSSARY

Court Cards—As with playing cards, these refer to the "court" figures in the full Tarot pack, four in this case (Page, Knight, Queen, and King) as opposed to three in regular playing cards.

Layout—*See* ***Spread***.

Major Arcana—The twenty-two Tarot Trumps. (The word *arcana* relates to mysteries or secrets.)

Marseilles (pack)—The most common form of traditional Tarot deck, prevalent over several centuries. The city of Marseilles was once a prominent center for Tarot manufacturing, hence the term, although some Marseilles-type cards were made in other European areas too. Note that there are alternative spellings: Marseille and Marseilles; the additional *s* is normally used in English.

Minchiate—An elite Tarot pack with ninety-seven cards, thought to originate in Florence in the sixteenth century. It is associated with a particular type of Tarot card game, and its imagery is more allegorical than that of the Marseilles pack.

Minor Arcana—The fifty-six suit cards of the full Tarot pack. *See also* ***Suits***.

Querent—The person who asks a question of the Tarot reader. It is a shorthand term to indicate the person who is on the receiving end of a Tarot interpretation.

Reader—The person who sets out the Tarot cards and interprets their meaning as a form of divination.

Reversal—The practice of shuffling the Tarot pack so that cards can appear upside-down or right-side up. The interpretation of reversed cards is usually a reevaluated form of their right-side up meaning, often with a more negative slant.

Significator—The first card drawn, usually representing either the person asking the question or the subject inquired about. Most Tarot layouts use a significator.

Spread—A chosen form in which to lay out Tarot cards to perform a reading. Usually, each position in the spread has its own significance; for example, as representing past or future or a particular department of life, such as love or aspirations.

Suits—The four fourteen-card sections of the Minor Arcana of the Tarot, which are usually called coins, cups, swords, and wands. They correspond to spades, hearts, diamonds, and clubs in modern-day playing cards.

Tarocchi—Usually used as a name for specific card games played with Tarot decks, or a version of the Tarot. These games are still popular in Italy and France and come in a variety of forms.

Triumphs—This term relates to the Italian word Trionfi, used to designate the twenty-two Tarot Trumps. It also corresponds to the Triumphs of processions that used to take place in Italy, with various tableaux representing conquering heroes and scenes of life, each one "triumph-ing" over or "trumping" the one before it.

Trumps—The usual word for the twenty-two Tarot cards of the Major Arcana, each a symbolic image open to interpretation on various levels. The term Trumps or Tri-umphs may relate to a kind of gaming sequence where one card "trumps" another. In Tarot reading, Tarot Trumps are generally considered to be of equal status.

ABOUT THE AUTHOR

Cherry Gilchrist is an award-winning author whose broad range of titles includes books both for adults and children, such as the popular *Stories from the Silk Road*, the well-known *Alchemy, the Great Work*, and the ground-breaking *Circle of Nine*. Many years of visiting Russia to research traditional culture there resulted in *The Soul of Russia*, also published as *Russian Magic*. Cherry is a long-term practitioner of the tarot, and she has researched its provenance, relating it to esoteric systems such as the Kabbalah, alchemy, and astrology. She holds degrees in English and Anthropology from Cambridge University and a postgraduate diploma in Cultural Astronomy and Astrology from Bath Spa University.

Cherry lives in Exeter, UK with her husband, artist Robert Lee-Wade. Visit her at *www.cherrygilchrist.co.uk*

TO OUR READERS

W eiser Books, an imprint of Red Wheel/Weiser, publishes books across the entire spectrum of occult, esoteric, speculative, and New Age subjects. Our mission is to publish quality books that will make a difference in people's lives without advocating any one particular path or field of study. We value the integrity, originality, and depth of knowledge of our authors.

Our readers are our most important resource, and we appreciate your input, suggestions, and ideas about what you would like to see published.

Visit our website at *www.redwheelweiser.com* to learn about our upcoming books and free downloads, and be sure to go to *www.redwheelweiser.com/newsletter* to sign up for newsletters and exclusive offers.

You can also contact us at *info@rwwbooks.com* or at

Red Wheel/Weiser, LLC
65 Parker, Suite 7
Newburyport, MA 01950